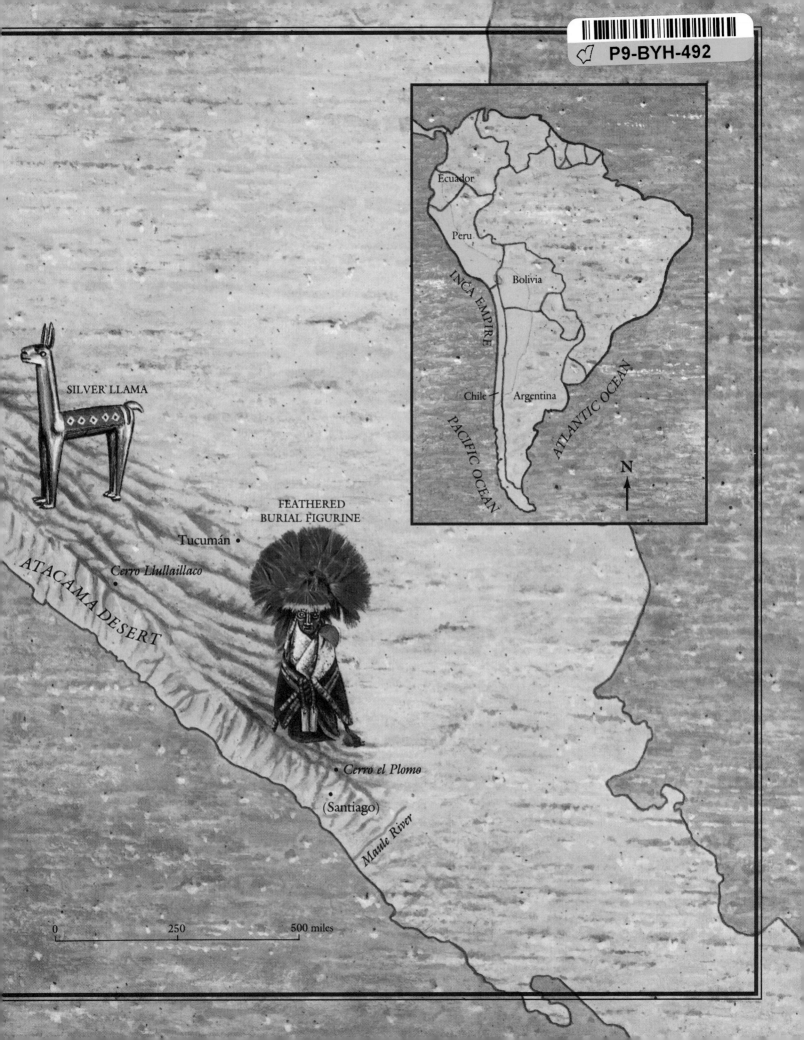

SILVER LLAMA

FEATHERED
BURIAL FIGURINE

Tucumán •

Cerro Llullaillaco •

ATACAMA DESERT

• *Cerro el Plomo*

• (Santiago)

Maule River

0   250   500 miles

Ecuador

Peru

INCA EMPIRE

Bolivia

Chile — Argentina

PACIFIC OCEAN

ATLANTIC OCEAN

N

Cover: His cheek bulging with a wad of coca, an Inca in a cloth turban peers out from a background of the ruins of the Andean city of Machu Picchu. The elongated earlobes, perforated to hold decorative disks, indicate that the man portrayed in this portion of a four-and-a-half-inch high, hammered gold statue was of high rank.

End paper: The map, painted by Paul Breeden, shows the Inca empire at its height in the early 16th century. It stretched more than 2,000 miles south from modern Ecuador, deep into Chile *(inset),* and inland from the arid coastal deserts along the Pacific to the far side of the snow-covered Andes. Breeden also painted the vignettes illustrating the timeline on pages 158-159.

INCAS:
LORDS OF GOLD
AND GLORY

Time-Life Books is a division of Time Life Inc., a wholly owned subsidiary of **THE TIME INC. BOOK COMPANY**

TIME-LIFE BOOKS

PRESIDENT: Mary N. Davis

MANAGING EDITOR: Thomas H. Flaherty
Director of Editorial Resources: Elise D. Ritter-Clough
Executive Art Director: Ellen Robling
Director of Photography and Research: John Conrad Weiser
Editorial Board: Dale M. Brown, Roberta Conlan, Laura Foreman, Lee Hassig, Jim Hicks, Blaine Marshall, Rita Thievon Mullin, Henry Woodhead
Assistant Director of Editorial Resources/Training Manager: Norma E. Shaw

PUBLISHER: Robert H. Smith

Associate Publisher: Ann M. Mirabito
Editorial Director: Russell B. Adams, Jr.
Marketing Director: Anne C. Everhart
Director of Production Services: Robert N. Carr
Production Manager: Prudence G. Harris
Supervisor of Quality Control: James King

Editorial Operations
Production: Celia Beattie
Library: Louise D. Forstall
Computer Composition: Deborah G. Tait (Manager), Monika D. Thayer, Janet Barnes Syring, Lillian Daniels
Interactive Media Specialist: Patti H. Cass

Library of Congress Cataloging in Publication Data
Incas: Lords of gold and glory / by the editors of Time-Life Books.
    p. cm.—(Lost civilizations)
Includes bibliographical references and index.
ISBN 0-8094-9870-7 (trade)
ISBN 0-8094-9871-5 (lib. bdg.)
1. Incas.   I. Time-Life Books. II. Series.
F3429.I6   1992
980'.01—dc20   92-5149

LOST CIVILIZATIONS

SERIES EDITOR: Dale M. Brown
Series Administrator: Philip Brandt George

Editorial staff for: *Incas: Lords of Gold and Glory*
Art Director: Barbara M. Sheppard
Picture Editor: Tina S. McDowell
Text Editors: Charlotte Anker, Robert Somerville
Associate Editors/Research: Denise Dersin, Patricia Mitchell
Assistant Art Director: Bill McKenney
Writers: Darcie Conner Johnston, James M. Lynch
Senior Copy Coordinator: Anne Farr
Picture Coordinator: Gail Feinberg
Editorial Assistant: Patricia D. Whiteford

Special Contributors: Tony Allan, Ronald H. Bailey, Beryl Lieff Benderly, John Cottrell, Kenneth C. Danforth, Donald Dale Jackson, M. Linda Lee (text); Paul Edholm, Ira Gitlin, Mary Grace Mayberry, Eugenia S. Scharf (research); Roy Nanovic (index)

Correspondents: Elisabeth Kraemer-Singh (Bonn), Christine Hinze (London), Christina Lieberman (New York), Maria Vincenza Aloisi (Paris), Ann Natanson (Rome). Valuable assistance was also provided by: Gay Kavanagh (Brussels); Barbara Gevene Hertz (Copenhagen); Adriana von Hagen (Lima); Judy Aspinall (London); Trini Bandrés (Madrid); Elizabeth Brown, Katheryn White (New York); Leonora Dodsworth (Rome); Robert Kroon (Zurich).

The Consultants:
Gordon F. McEwan is associate curator and head of the Department of New World Art at the Denver Museum. He has extensive curatorial, teaching, and field research experience in ancient Peruvian archaeology, specializing in the valley of Cuzco and the origins of the Incas and their empire.

Michael E. Moseley, professor of anthropology at the University of Florida at Gainesville, provided invaluable assistance with the "Artisans of the Empire" essay in this volume. Professor Moseley has more than 25 years' experience as an active archaeologist in Peru and is the author of *The Inca and Their Ancestors.*

R. Tom Zuidema, author of numerous articles and books on Andean cultural history and a recognized expert on Huaman Poma and his chronicle, is a professor of anthropology at the University of Illinois at Urbana.

Other Publications:

ECHOES OF GLORY
THE NEW FACE OF WAR
HOW THINGS WORK
WINGS OF WAR
CREATIVE EVERYDAY COOKING
COLLECTOR'S LIBRARY OF THE UNKNOWN
CLASSICS OF WORLD WAR II
TIME-LIFE LIBRARY OF CURIOUS AND UNUSUAL FACTS
AMERICAN COUNTRY
VOYAGE THROUGH THE UNIVERSE
THE THIRD REICH
THE TIME-LIFE GARDENER'S GUIDE
MYSTERIES OF THE UNKNOWN
TIME FRAME
FIX IT YOURSELF
FITNESS, HEALTH & NUTRITION
SUCCESSFUL PARENTING
HEALTHY HOME COOKING
UNDERSTANDING COMPUTERS
LIBRARY OF NATIONS
THE ENCHANTED WORLD
THE KODAK LIBRARY OF CREATIVE PHOTOGRAPHY
GREAT MEALS IN MINUTES
THE CIVIL WAR
PLANET EARTH
COLLECTOR'S LIBRARY OF THE CIVIL WAR
THE EPIC OF FLIGHT
THE GOOD COOK
WORLD WAR II
HOME REPAIR AND IMPROVEMENT
THE OLD WEST

For information on and a full description of any of the Time-Life Books series listed above, please call 1-800-621-7026 or write:
Reader Information
Time-Life Customer Service
P.O. Box C-32068
Richmond, Virginia 23261-2068

This volume is one in a series that explores the worlds of the past, using the finds of archaeologists and other scientists to bring ancient peoples and their cultures vividly to life.

Other volumes include:

Egypt: Land of the Pharaohs
Aztecs: Reign of Blood & Splendor
Pompeii: The Vanished City

INCAS:
LORDS OF GOLD
AND GLORY

By the Editors of Time-Life Books

TIME-LIFE BOOKS, ALEXANDRIA, VIRGINIA

CONTENTS

A VIOLENT CLASH OF ALIEN CULTURES

A silver alpaca, used as a ceremonial offering, honors the woolly animal that thrived on the steep slopes of the Andes, made habitable and productive by the Incas through terracing. The giant stepped fields at Machu Picchu give eloquent testimony to the skill of the empire's engineers.

Hiram Bingham was not going to let a little bad weather stop him; still, it was not until 10 o'clock that he emerged from his tent that drizzly morning of July 24, 1911, deep in the heart of the Peruvian Andes. The night before, a local tavernkeeper—if such a name can be used to describe someone with so humble an establishment as his—had teased the explorer's imagination with a report of nearby Inca ruins. But as the tall, thin man stood inspecting the rain-swollen torrent noisily surging through the canyon of the Urubamba River, he was none too hopeful. He knew that similar reports had already led him to nothing more exciting than a few courses of ancient masonry, where some half-buried hut lay. Yet such disappointments had not deflected him from his overriding purpose—which was to find the lost city of Vilcabamba, known from historical records to be the final stronghold of the Incas. There, in semi-isolation, these proud lords of the Andes had maintained for nearly 35 years a rump kingdom in defiance of the Spaniards, vanquishers of their once-mighty empire.

Bingham had been helped in his search by a recently discovered autobiographical chronicle, dictated by one of the last Inca rulers, that provided new clues to Vilcabamba's location. His hunch was that the fabled refuge lay hidden in this densely forested valley, "designed by nature," he mused, "as a sanctuary for the oppressed."

A man of multiple interests, the 35-year-old adventurer, who taught Latin American history at Yale University, his alma mater, had come to Peru to study its history, botany, and geography. His keen enthusiasm, springing from an earlier visit to the country, had spawned the expedition he now headed, funded by Yale and some of his rich former classmates.

Only three weeks earlier Bingham and his team had set out from Cuzco, the ancient Inca capital, to explore the mountainous realm to the northwest, where Andean peaks soar to heights of up to 18,000 feet. The conduit here, leading from one region to the other, is the Urubamba River, which cuts a deep valley down into the dense Amazon rain forest. The area's sharply angled slopes, some of them sheer rock, and dense vegetation had discouraged travelers from straying far from its few, difficult roads. Bingham had the advantage of a new route that had been blasted along the riverbank two years previously. By traversing it, he had arrived at this wild and desolate spot, 7,000 feet above sea level. "In the variety of its charms and the power of its spell, I know of no place in the world which can compare with it," he was to write. "Not only has it great snow peaks looming above the clouds more than two miles overhead, gigantic precipices of many-colored granite rising sheer for thousands of feet above the foaming, glistening, roaring rapids; it has also, in striking contrast, orchids and tree ferns, the delectable beauty of luxurious vegetation, and the mysterious witchery of the jungle."

The explorer had listened attentively when the tavernkeeper had spoken of Inca ruins located on the saddle of an upthrusting ridge across the river from the expedition's campsite. Jotting down the names of this mountain's two peaks in his notebook—Huayna Picchu and Machu Picchu—he persuaded the reluctant tavernkeeper to lead him to the place with the promise of a silver dollar. But now, with rain falling, his colleagues—who were skeptical of the peasant's story—already had their minds set on washing shirts and perhaps hunting butterflies, and declined to go with Bingham. Thus while his teammates remained behind in the relative comfort of camp, Bingham set out in the drizzle, in the company of only the guide and a government-appointed bodyguard.

They hiked to an improvised bridge of long, spindly tree trunks, lashed together with vines, that stretched precariously

Hiram Bingham's barefoot Indian guide, Melchor Arteaga, crosses a makeshift log bridge above the turbulent Urubamba River in this photograph shot by the explorer on July 24, 1911. Moments later, Bingham himself would crawl across, terrified, on his way to the discovery of Machu Picchu, another 2,000 feet above the river valley. In his journal, he tersely noted the time, subject, and shutter speed of this, his second photograph of the day: "10:45. #2. Bridge. 1/25."

across rocks in the rushing Urubamba. A single misstep and a man could fall in. "No one could live for an instant in the icy cold rapids," Bingham recalled. As his companions gingerly made their way barefoot over the bridge, Bingham got down on his hands and knees and crawled across, six inches at a time. On the opposite bank the trio mounted a steep trail, grasping vines to ascend the slippery rocks, and keeping an anxious eye out for the poisonous yellow fer-de-lance snakes known to infest the area. After climbing about 2,000 feet, they arrived at the hut of a Peruvian family. The tavern-keeper thought better about continuing, choosing instead to stay behind and gossip with the hut's owner, while Bingham and his guard continued upward, led now by a little boy not 10 years old.

After rounding a promontory and climbing a steeply terraced hillside dating from Inca times, Bingham was rewarded for his efforts. "Suddenly I found myself confronted with the walls of ruined houses built of the finest quality of Inca stonework," he was to write later. "It was hard to see them for they were partly covered with trees and moss, the growth of centuries, but in the dense shadow, hiding in bamboo thickets and tangled vines, appeared here and there walls of white granite ashlars carefully cut and exquisitely fitted together *(pages 35-45)*." Bingham could hardly believe his good fortune as he wandered among the overgrown ruins, encountering wonder after wonder—a royal mausoleum, a temple to the sun, more magnificent temples, a broad plaza, dozens of houses. "It seemed like an unbelievable dream," he exulted.

Yet was this Vilcabamba? He could not be certain. But now, his enthusiasm fired up by his find, he determined to continue his search for the lost city. The next morning the explorer broke camp, and in the course of several days of arduous trekking, stumbled upon a series of imposing ruins, including an urban site vaster in size than

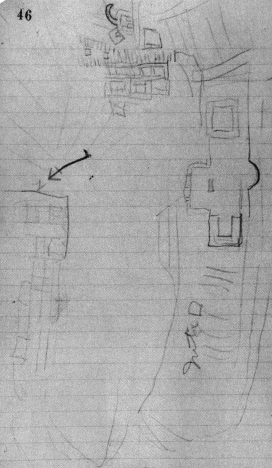

his earlier discovery, Machu Picchu, and buried under centuries of tangled growth in an area known as Espíritu Pampa. Though it lay only 60 miles east of Machu Picchu, it was 6,000 feet lower down and difficult of access. Returning to Yale after a couple of fruitful months in the field, Bingham tentatively identified this lowlands place as his Vilcabamba, for indeed passages in the documentary evidence he had examined seemed to suggest just such a tropical location.

Yet it was Machu Picchu, nestled between the Andean peaks, that lured Bingham back for a longer stay the following year, under the joint auspices of Yale University and the National Geographic Society. Spending the summer of 1912 clearing the stone ruins, he became convinced that this picturesque citadel—and not the mysterious city buried in the jungle—was Vilcabamba, after all. Ironically, scholarly opinion now supports Bingham's original thinking.

Accessible today from Cuzco by a railway that follows the route Bingham took in 1911, the mountain retreat of Machu Picchu, built 100 years before the Spanish conquest for a ruler called Pachacuti Inca Yupanqui, has become the best-known ruin of the fabulous Inca civilization. At the apex of their power in the early 16th century, the Incas, an aristocracy of a few thousand individuals, all members of a single ethnic group, ruled one of the largest empires of the era. Their territory stretched for more than 2,500 miles down almost the entire length of the Andes, from the southern border of

En route to Machu Picchu in 1911, Hiram Bingham poses with his mule. Among his belongings he carried a leatherbound notebook (above), in which he scribbled the details of his adventure: the weather and topography, his impressions of each of the retreat's stone edifices, a crude map of the site—and the sequence in which he took his photographs, the first ever to be shot of the forgotten city, made with a Kodak 4 x 5 camera (right).

today's Colombia to what is today Santiago, Chile, incorporating all of present-day Ecuador and Peru as well as parts of Bolivia and northwest Argentina. Its heartland lay on the precipitous spine of the Andes, the world's second-highest mountain range after the Himalayas. Its eastern boundaries touched the rain forest of the Amazon headwaters and its western, the sands of the bleak coastal deserts. The Incas called this domain Tahuantinsuyu, the "land of the four quarters," a name reflecting the segments into which the empire was officially divided, with Cuzco at its center. Within it—and very much under the Incas' thumb—lived an estimated seven to nine million people comprising as many as 100 ethnic groups.

Defying conventional assumptions about what made highly developed civilizations possible, the extraordinary Incas succeeded without benefit of wheeled transport or writing. Through sheer will power and the application of their keen intelligence to the harnessing of human energy, they created in less than 100 years one of the most intricately organized societies the world has known. But the meteoric rise of the Incas was followed by their even more precipitous fall. Tahuantinsuyu was ruled by a succession of great warrior-kings, each of whom was known, in his reign, as the Sapa Inca, the "sole Inca" or "unique one." Extending their rule over an expanding territory, these monarchs gained a prestige that led their subjects to accord them the exalted title Son of Inti—Inti being the Inca sun god—as well as the deference and riches due such status.

Yet for all its power, this imposing civilization was conquered in short order by fewer than 200 Spaniards. The invaders' courage and even their advanced weaponry might have amounted to little against so formidable and numerous a foe had events been different.

But it was the Incas' fate that the Spaniards would be aided in their victory by events taking place within the empire itself.

Rumors of a land of gold had long been circulating among Spaniards in the New World in the early 16th century, and hearsay evidence indicated that it lay somewhere south of the equator. Tempted by such talk, a veteran of Spain's Italian campaigns named Francisco Pizarro decided to find out the truth for himself. Illegitimate and illiterate, he had come to the New World in 1502 to seek his fortune. He saw seven years' hard service in the Caribbean, where he helped suppress the Taino Indians on the island of Hispaniola, today's Dominican Republic and Haiti. In 1513 he accompanied Vasco Núñez de Balboa across the Isthmus of Panama to become one of the first Europeans to behold the Pacific Ocean. Settling down in Panama, he became a landowner, was given a quota of Indian workers, and grew to be quite well-off. But such success left him restless. Joining forces with Diego de Almagro, another soldier of fortune, and Hernando de Luque, a priest, they put together an expedition that in 1524 would take them from Panama on a difficult and frustrating journey into the unexplored territory to the south.

A second expedition launched in 1526, on which Pizarro bartered for gold, provided enough of a glimpse of riches to inspire him with dreams of wealth and glory. One of his ships captured a group of Inca traders on a raft of balsa wood borne by sails of finely woven cotton. The Spaniards shrewdly held three of the captives to be trained as interpreters, setting the others free. "They were carrying many pieces of silver and gold as personal ornaments," Pizarro later reported to his emperor, Charles V, and he went on to whet the ruler's appetite by listing some of the items—among them, "crowns and diadems, belts and bracelets, armor for the legs and breastplates; tweezers and rattles and strings and clusters of beads and rubies."

This expedition was even more arduous than the first, leading many of his men to despair as hunger, disease, and death overtook them. But Pizarro would not be deterred by adversity. He pulled out his sword and drew a line in the sand. "Comrades and friends," he said, pointing to one side, "there lies the part that represents death, hardship, hunger, nakedness, rains, and abandonment; this side represents comfort. Here, you return to Panama to be poor; there, you may go on to Peru to be rich. Choose which becomes you as good Spaniards." Thirteen elected to remain with their leader, and for this they came to be known as "the 13 of glory."

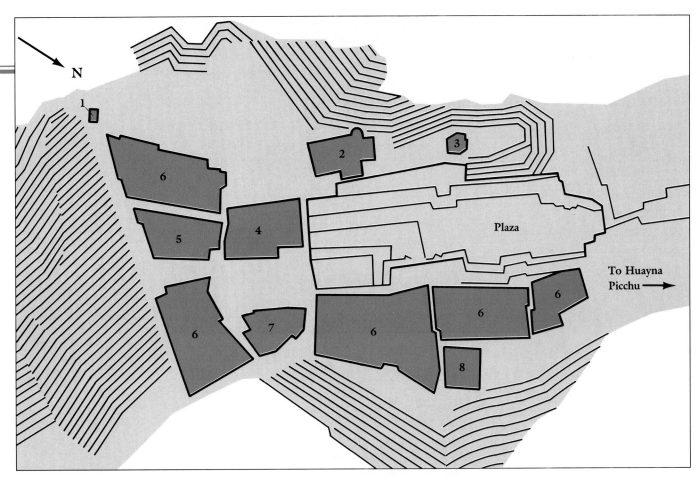

As is revealed by this schematic map based on Bingham's hypothetical identification of sites, terraces fall away from the spine of the Andes, where a grassy plaza divides Machu Picchu into two wards. The city gate (1) permits entrance at the southern end, near the Sacred Plaza temples (2) and the intihuatana (3), *the large stone where Incas worshiped the sun god. The palace known as the King's Group (4) and the temple called El Torreón (5) are among the finest of the 200 or so stone buildings, which also include clusters of small houses (6), so-called prisons (7), and storehouses (8). Huayna Picchu looms at the city's northern edge.*

In 1527, Pizarro reached the Inca town of Tumbes. There the Spaniards were greeted with friendly curiosity by the town's inhabitants, who told them of temples inland, sheathed in precious metals, and of gardens where living plants grew alongside finely crafted replicas of gold and silver. Such accounts further stoked Pizarro's desire. Lacking neither the manpower nor the resources to attempt an immediate invasion of Inca territory, he determined to return at the head of a conquering force in the near future. But despite the lure of riches to come, it would take three years and a trip to Spain before all the necessary arrangements could be made.

In his home country, Pizarro had proudly told Charles V of his discoveries and of the Inca treasure that could be theirs for the taking. Excited by the prospect of territorial and financial gain, Charles bestowed on the adventurer the right to explore and conquer this hitherto unknown empire on the other side of the world. Pizarro was to have the title of governor and captain-general in the lands that came under his control. As would soon become apparent to Pizarro and his cohorts, the delay in setting out, frustrating though it had been, actually worked to their advantage.

The story of the Incas' tragic downfall is known mainly from the reports of the Spaniards. With the notable exception of Pizarro,

the conquistadors—among whose ranks was Hernando de Soto—had a high degree of literacy, and the records they left behind offer eyewitness descriptions of the first encounters between the two civilizations. Once the conquest was accomplished, other, more sympathetic, recorders followed, who used the knowledge they gleaned from the Incas themselves to describe Inca traditions. From both sets of accounts and the observations of conscientious civil servants sent to the new colony by Spanish rulers, ethnohistorians have been able to piece together a picture of the Incas during their last days. It is a sad one.

In 1524, when the empire of the Incas was at the height of its glory, rumors arrived at the Sapa Inca's court of extraordinary events. "Floating fortresses" had sailed along the northern coast bearing strangers with white skin and hair on their faces, who came to be called "the bearded ones." The news was disturbing to many; in later years, Inca nobles told a Spanish chronicler that the Sapa Inca himself, a great warrior named Huayna Capac, had seen the danger and foretold that one day the strangers would threaten his throne.

Within a year or two the Sapa Inca was dead. Although it is impossible to verify the disease that carried him off, it seems likely that it was smallpox, introduced to the Americas by the conquistadors. Outpacing the conquerors, this illness reached native peoples even in lands the Spaniards had yet to explore and probably arrived in western South America by 1525, from the Caribbean via Venezuela and Colombia, where the Europeans already had a foothold. The disease spread so quickly among the Incas, who had no immunity to it, that armies were decimated and entire families stricken. It has been said of smallpox that a cup of water offered at the right moment can save a life, but often there was no one well enough to provide the dying a drink. Morale plummeted among survivors, most

Embroiled in a fierce battle against each other for the supreme position of Sapa Inca, royal brothers Huascar (above, left) and Atahualpa—illustrated in watercolors from a 16th-century Spanish album—plunged the Inca empire into chaos. Arriving in the thick of the civil war in 1532, the conquistadors exploited their enmity—and ultimately annihilated the civilization. The Spaniards believed their actions were "to the glory of God, because we have conquered and brought to our holy Catholic faith so vast a number of heathens, aided by His holy guidance."

Driven by lust for gold and dreams of glory, the Spanish adventurer Francisco Pizarro—shown in battle regalia in this 19th-century painting—conquered and looted the rich Inca empire with an army of fewer than 200 men. In 1541, at the age of 63, he was stabbed to death by supporters of his one-time ally, Diego de Almagro, whom Pizarro's brother Hernando had executed after the two rivals warred for supremacy of Peru.

of whom had lost numerous relatives and friends. Not only did the epidemic kill Huayna Capac; it also carried off his probable heir, setting the stage for strife.

It was customary for the Sapa Inca to nominate his successor. Although the honor normally devolved on one of the sons of his principal wife, the Coya, it was not necessarily the eldest who was chosen, but rather the one considered most fit to rule. A new Sapa Inca, Huascar—whose name, "gentle hummingbird," should not be taken as a reflection of either his character or his stature—was proclaimed successor in Cuzco by the Inca nobles there.

Much of the court was not in Cuzco, however, but in the northern city of Quito, which Huayna Capac had conquered, and where he had elected to spend the latter years of his life. It was there that trouble began. Quito had become almost a second capital, splitting the hitherto united leaders of the empire into two contending factions. The army, which was quartered in Quito, preferred another son of Huayna Capac, Atahualpa—whose name means wild turkey cock, a bird that commanded respect in the Andes. He had more than proved himself, having spent most of his life at his father's side in the field of battle.

One Spanish veteran described Atahualpa as being "of fine person, of medium size, not too fat, beautiful of face and grave, with red eyes, a man much feared by his people." As evidence of the impact his bearing had on people, this observer described seeing an important nobleman "tremble in such a manner that he could not stand upon his feet" in the royal presence for fear he may have displeased the ruler. The dread was not entirely irrational; Atahualpa could be ruthless. He also showed a quick intelligence that impressed the Spaniards, who noted how quickly he became an expert at chess.

Although he had repeatedly proclaimed his loyalty to the new Sapa Inca, Atahualpa knew that Huascar must view him as a rival. Alert to the possibility that one of his brother's supporters might try to assassinate him if he left his power base in Quito, he ignored every effort to persuade him to come to Cuzco to pay his respects. For five uneasy years a standoff endured. Finally, Huascar brought events to a head by demanding his brother's presence. When Atahualpa again failed to appear, sending ambassadors bearing gifts in his place, Huascar—egged on by courtiers hostile to his brother—had the emissaries tortured and killed, then sent an army to bring Atahualpa to Cuzco by force. Angered, Atahualpa called his faction to arms, and the land—already mourning the loss of so many of its citizens to the smallpox epidemic—soon found itself in the throes of a civil war.

It was a blood-drenched conflict with no quarter given, and it set in motion the process of destruction that European invasion would subsequently complete. At first Huascar's men were successful, and Atahualpa was captured. He escaped, however, and joined his army. Meeting his former captors in battle, Atahualpa defeated them; following Inca military custom, he had the skull of the opposing commander, another brother, lined with gold and turned into a drinking vessel, and his skin made into a drum. Huascar dispatched a second army; but his raw troops proved no match for the veterans surrounding Atahualpa, and, in a two-day battle, they were defeated.

Now it was Atahualpa's turn to take the offensive. His generals marched south toward Cuzco. They met a third royal army recruited to protect the city. This time Huascar's men seized the initiative; they set brush fires that broke up the enemy lines and drove the soldiers from the field. Regrouping, Atahualpa's generals prepared an ambush in a ravine near the battlefield. It netted the greatest prize of all—Huascar himself, captured alive. His army was subsequently routed, and Atahualpa's men entered Cuzco in triumph.

They showed no mercy to the defeated enemy. Tied to a frame, Huascar was forced to watch while his numerous wives were butchered. His friends and advisers were also slaughtered, and their remains left tied to poles lining a road out of the city as a bloody warning of the danger of thwarting Atahualpa's will. Huascar was held prisoner in the fortress of Jauja, there to await his fate.

It was during this period of upheaval, in 1532, that Pizarro and Almagro, who had accompanied him on the two previous expeditions, returned to the town of Tumbes. This time Pizarro had with him some 160 adventurers, 67 of whom were horsemen, and an assortment of weapons, including muskets, crossbows, pikes, lances, and artillery, supplied by Charles V. He found not the prosperous city he had earlier visited but a devastated ruin; like much of the Inca empire, it had suffered grievously in the course of the civil war and had been ravaged by smallpox. While the sight disheartened Pizarro's men, their commander was shrewd enough to realize that the Indians' misfortune could be the Spaniards' gain. Lingering for five months near the coast, sustained in part by the looting of the em-

This skull—probably the remains of a defeated opponent—may once have been lined with gold and used for chicha, *a beer most often brewed from corn. Such skull cups served as symbols of victory for Inca leaders who triumphed in battle.*

peror's storehouses there, Pizarro sought to find out what he could about the state of Inca affairs. When news came that Atahualpa was encamped at Cajamarca, less than a fortnight's march away from him, he set off into the interior with his tiny army, a few Indian lackeys, and two Indian translators whom he had taken from the raft some years previously.

It was a desperate, almost mad enterprise. Indeed, nine of Pizarro's men, daunted by the prospect of entering the mountainous domain of the Inca, turned back. The rest of the little band pressed forward, climbing ever higher, crossing raging torrents on perilously narrow suspension bridges made of ropes of ichu grass slung from stone pilasters. They could not help being impressed by the evidence of Inca engineering skills all around them, including flagstone-paved roads, bordered with shade-giving trees, with water running in stone channels alongside for the convenience of travelers. "Such magnificent roads can be seen nowhere in Christendom, in country as rough as this," one of them conceded.

While the Spaniards pursued their arduous upward trek, the thin air of the heights making it harder and harder for them to breathe, the victorious Atahualpa was resting with his army at Cajamarca, favored by Inca rulers for its healthful hot springs. Earlier he had received word that the bearded white men, whose advent had troubled his father, had returned in their wooden ships. Soon runners from the coast informed him that the strangers were moving inland. Atahualpa responded by sending an envoy to invite Pizarro and his men to visit him. The report the Inca ambassador carried back to his master contained the first of a series of fatal misreadings of Spanish intentions. As Atahualpa later revealed, the emissary told him the bearded ones were not fighting men, and that 200 Incas would be sufficient to restrain them, if indeed they posed a threat. The Inca could not have known that Pizarro had fostered such an assessment by receiving the ambassador in a courtly manner, giving him a shirt and two goblets of Venetian glass, and talking of peace. Consequently, the little army of strangers was allowed to march unmolested through the mountains.

The Spaniards panted in their armor up tracks that clung vertiginously to soaring mountainsides. Forced to dismount by the steepness of the ascent, the troopers led their horses, weighted down with cannons, armaments, and supplies, along paths so narrow that a single false step could have sent men and beasts plunging to their death down condor-haunted ravines. They found the commanding heights dominated menacingly by stone fortresses, which, to the exhausted soldiers' relief, turned out to be unmanned.

After a week in the mountains, Pizarro's army descended upon the valley of Cajamarca on November 15, only to be greeted by an alarming sight. According to one eyewitness, so numerous were the Inca warriors scattered on the hillside "that we were filled with fright. We never thought the Indians could occupy such a proud position, nor so many tents, so well set up. It filled all us Spaniards with confusion and fear. But we dared not show it, much less turn back, for if they sensed the least weakness in us, the very Indians we brought with us would have killed us."

Pizarro quartered his men in the main square, an open space surrounded on three sides by long buildings, each with several doors. He dispatched a group of horsemen led by Hernando de Soto to pay his respects to Atahualpa and to lure him to a meeting. Tense but resolute, the Spanish envoys rode through the silent ranks of the Inca army along a paved road to the royal residence, located near the hot springs a few miles from the town. In the courtyard of the royal palace, "a pool had been made, and two pipes of water, one hot and one cold, entered it; the two pipes came from springs," one of the men later reported. There they found the new ruler sitting on a golden stool, "with all the majesty in the world, surrounded by all his women and with many chiefs near him."

A war of nerves was played out between the two parties. Atahualpa had sought to impress Pizarro with the military might at his command, and he had succeeded. The Spaniards, too, tried to disconcert their opponents. Understanding how remarkable horses seemed to the Indians, who themselves had no domestic animals larger than llamas, de Soto charged straight at Atahualpa, then pulled up his mount so close to him that the tasseled fringe the monarch wore as a crown was stirred by its breath, while froth from its mouth dripped on his clothing. But Atahualpa sat immobile, a perfect model of the Inca warrior in the face of danger. He expected similar fortitude from his followers; those who flinched he later had executed.

Atahualpa remained silent for a while, then addressed the newcomers through one of the interpreters they had brought with them. He chided the Spaniards for having robbed his storehouses of

EXPLORER GENE SAVOY AND THE LOST CITIES OF THE ANDES

Often hidden out of sight, covered by jungle, or perched on distant peaks, seemingly well beyond reach, some—but not all—of the lost cities of the ancient Andean peoples have revealed themselves to a few hearty individuals with the patience, fortitude, and wherewithal to go look for them. The American explorer Gene Savoy *(below)* is one such person, and in the three decades that he has been trekking through the Andes, he has found more than 40 previously unknown settlements that tell excitingly of the societies that built them, then vanished.

Savoy had long been fascinated by Vilcabamba, the last stronghold of the Incas. Attempts to locate it had not been successful. As far back as 1834, the French Count de Sartiges endured weeks of exhaustion and thirst searching for the ruins. Other intrepid souls followed, each, in turn, certain he had found the elusive city. In 1912, Hiram Bingham joined the ranks when he declared Machu Picchu to be the Incas' final refuge. Although for the next 50 years most scholars accepted his claim, not everyone was convinced. On the heels of a failed attempt by a 1963 American team that parachuted deep into unexplored jungle, Gene Savoy set out for the most likely site, one, ironically, that Bingham had stumbled on but dismissed, 93 miles northwest of Cuzco.

Savoy had prepared himself well, having carefully studied historical chronicles for clues, gotten the backing of the Peruvian government, and assembled a support team. After days of struggling through the thick vegetation of mountain rain forests, Savoy and his men came upon the city at last. "We couldn't believe our eyes," he remembers. The ruins, situated between two

Gene Savoy, head of the Andean Explorers Foundation and Ocean Sailing Club, is shown here en route to Gran Vilaya, a forgotten city he found in Peru's forbidding Chachapoyas region. The map inset at right, which was drafted by his team's own cartographer, details the area of discovery.

rivers on a flat alluvial plain covered by trees and vines, occupied an area of approximately two square miles.

Not an archaeologist, Savoy would leave the digging to others. And soon he had set his sights on a search for another lost city, one he would call Gran Vilaya. "I was sure of one thing," Savoy writes. "Something did exist in the eastern jungles, but no one had managed to find it." At Vilcabamba, he had seen circular buildings that he believed were the work of the Chachapoyas, a people who had inhabited the northernmost reaches of Peru. Their domain, some 500 miles northwest of Vilcabamba, lay 8,000 to 10,000 feet above sea level in cloud-wreathed mountains and dense rain forest. The region was so remote that the Incas supposedly added the kingdom to their empire only in 1480, taking, it is thought, 40 years to subdue the inhabitants. With its suffocating jungle growth, almost perpetual rain, and lack of human habitation, the area had deterred archaeologists for decades.

In 1965, Savoy's team traced by air Inca roads leading from Vilcabamba into the Chachapoyas kingdom. It took a preliminary expedition days to locate the first ruins, 9,400 feet above sea level. Savoy named this site Gran Pajatén, after the famous colonial ruins of Pajatén nearby. There the team explored a complex of slate-and-mortar circular structures, many of which were covered with mosaic-like stone figures of humans, animals, and birds, apparently condors (*background*).

One day, while flying in a helicopter, Savoy and some of his teammates spotted caves in cliff faces relatively close to Gran Pajatén. Amazingly, three-foot-high wood carvings, found in the caves, were still in fine condition, despite centuries of exposure to the humidity. As a follow-up, a ground-survey team pursued Inca roads 90 miles northwest and came upon dozens of cliff tombs with mummy cases

Gran Pajatén's main circular structure, shown at left, stands on a platform and measures 45 feet in diameter and about 12 feet in height. Its façade is divided in half by a molding, and its upper sections are covered with geometrical friezes. Roots and vines wrapped around the ornamental stonework threaten to topple the giant structure, which perhaps may once have been a temple.

Gran Pajatén's imposing ruins are composed of thousands of individual stones fitted compactly together like those shown above. The human figures on the left are made from long black slate blocks. One head is crowned with sunburstlike rays; the other two have wings.

standing in rows inside the caves *(background)*. Some had been shot down by looters, and the shattered casings and their spilled contents of bone and textile lay on the earth below. Suspecting that this was a Chachapoyas necropolis, Savoy named the site Pueblo de los Muertos—City of the Dead. Systematic exploration revealed seven similar sites within a 40-square-mile area.

Abandoning the Chachapoyas region for more accessible areas, Savoy would not return for 15 years. This time he was determined to find the administrative center of the Chachapoyas, mentioned by Spanish chroniclers, and accompanied by almost 100 machete men, 70 mules, and 20 crew members, he did. It turned out to be a collection of linked settlements sprawling through 100 square miles of rain forest alive with the sound of monkeys and parrots. Over the next five years, he led eight expeditions into the area, exploring thousands of architectural remains that were perched on some 40 major mountaintops, with the peaks connected by broken roads. Among the ruins were what may well have been administrative buildings, temples, dwellings, and a network of ridge-top fortifications. "Gran Vilaya," says Savoy, who named the site after a nearby river canyon, may prove to be "the largest pre-Columbian city of the Americas. Its ruins dwarf Cuzco and everything the Incas ever built."

Gran Vilaya is certainly Savoy's most spectacular find and has been a magnet to archaeologists, who hope eventually to solve its many mysteries. As to what else may lie out there in the jungles, still awaiting discovery, Savoy has a ready answer: "Plenty."

These anthropomorphic mummy cases were once decorated with paints in vivid colors. Made with mud and vegetable fiber, the cases are believed to contain the remains of rulers.

At Diablo Huasi, just south of Pueblo de los Muertos, dozens of tombs mark the cliff face. One cave contained numerous mummies with their knees drawn up to their chests, wrapped in a netlike material, and surrounded by grave goods. As is their policy, Savoy's group left the cave undisturbed for the archaeologists.

Gran Vilaya is made up of thousands of white limestone structures like these. The buildings, many of which stand on terraces, range up to 40 feet in height and between 25 to 30 feet in diameter.

"some of my father's cloth" on entering the country and for having treated several of his chiefs badly. The conquistadors responded by boasting of their prowess as soldiers, disparaging some coastal Indians with whom they had actually fought for behaving "like women," and adding that one horse would have been enough to conquer their "entire land." But, cagily, the Spaniards also offered to apply their military acumen on behalf of Atahualpa. Before the brief encounter came to an end, Atahualpa, in his second tragic misjudgment, agreed to come to Cajamarca the next day to visit Pizarro.

That night was an anxious one for the Spaniards. Gazing out over the Inca campfires, "as thick as the stars of heaven," in the words of one soldier, they realized there was no turning back. Throughout the night they prayed and confessed their sins to their priests.

The two camps lay in wait for dawn, each led by a veteran warrior seeking personal legitimacy within the empire he served. Atahualpa wanted most of all to be officially crowned god-king of the Incas, thereby eliminating the challenge of his imprisoned half brother. The humbly born Pizarro, for his part, hoped that by becoming governor of Spain's newest colony he would at last attain prestige and acclaim. Each, on the morrow, would face a decisive encounter with an alien world. Pizarro, however, had an advantage: For years, he had dealt with peoples of the New World, studying their strengths and weaknesses. And his lessons in conquest had come from the master himself when, in Spain, he had listened to Hernán Cortés, his cousin, tell the story of how he had wrested Mexico from the Aztecs. Atahualpa, while able to muster hundreds of thousands of fierce, battle-hardened fighters, knew nothing of the European character.

At this key moment Pizarro decisively stamped the mark of his leadership on his forces. Uncouth and callous though he may have been, no one ever accused him of lacking courage. It has been reported that he was pleased by his men's desperation, which he deemed a welcome spur to the fighting he envisaged. "Make fortresses of your hearts, for you have no other," he told them. Based on the example of Cortés, who had conquered the mighty Aztec empire by kidnapping its emperor, he prepared an ambush.

Meanwhile, Atahualpa was plotting his own military strategy. Overnight, he sent 5,000 soldiers under command of his general, Rumiñavi, to seal off the road north of Cajamarca. His plan, he later told the Spaniards, was to take Pizarro and his men alive and sacrifice them to Inti, the sun god, retaining their horses for breeding. At dawn the next day, Pizarro stationed his forces within the buildings around the square to await Atahualpa's arrival. As morning turned to afternoon, the waiting told on the nerves of the massively outnumbered soldiers. Later, one recorded, "I have heard that many of the Spaniards made water without knowing it out of sheer terror."

Finally, at sunset, the imperial cortege approached. It seems that Atahualpa chose the time believing that the Spaniards were unable to ride horses in the dark. He provided a magnificent spectacle, and an intimidating one. On a wooden litter, lined with multicolored parrot feathers and decorated with jewel-encrusted silver and gold plates, Atahualpa was carried aloft by 80 retainers dressed in blue tunics, their badge of honor. Wearing a collar of emeralds over a robe woven with golden threads, the monarch held a gold shield emblazoned with an image of the sun.

"All the Indians wore gold and silver disks like crowns on their heads," one awed Spaniard later recorded. "In front was a squadron of Indians wearing a livery of checkered colors like a chessboard." Musicians played flutes, drums, and conch-shell trumpets to accompany dancers and choral groups who, as they marched, sang a song of praise to Atahualpa: "O great and very powerful Lord, Son of the Sun, only ruler, may all the earth obey you." One Spaniard recalled that it was "by no means lacking in grace for us who heard it." But another soldier remembered that it "sounded like the songs of hell."

Atahualpa had left the body of his army—some 80,000 men— outside the town, but his personal retinue nonetheless comprised upward of 5,000 warriors. Amazingly, they arrived unarmed, in ceremonial rather than in military array. Entering the square, they found it empty but for the odd figure of a robed Dominican friar, bearing a cross in one hand and a Bible in the other. The royal council in Spain had specified that heathens should be given the chance to accept Christianity voluntarily before there was any recourse to bloodshed, and the conquistadors were eager not to break the letter of the law. As the friar expounded the Christian faith to the bemused ruler, the translator told him that he was being asked to convert to the religion of the strangers. "You say your god was put to death, but my god," Atahualpa replied, pointing to the setting sun, "still lives."

He took the missal handed to him, at first showing interest in the writing it contained. He understood that it was believed by the

Spaniards to be what the Incas called a *huaca*, a talisman in which resided the spirit of the gods. Yet it may have seemed a flimsy token compared with the great stone huacas the Incas worshiped, and he dismissed it, throwing it to the ground. "This says nothing to me," he said contemptuously. The friar turned to Pizarro and is reputed to have said to him and his men: "Throw yourselves upon them forthwith. I give you all absolution."

Pizarro gave the signal for the attack. Two cannons fired into the massed Indians. The Spanish horsemen charged out of the buildings in their armor, cutting a swath through the ranks of unarmed men. The foot soldiers followed to the sound of blaring trumpets, rending the air with their battle cry of "Santiago," the name of the saint who the Spaniards believed aided them in battle.

The focus of the attack was Atahualpa himself. His nobles sought to protect him, but, unfamiliar with the sharpness of honed steel, many lost their hands to the slice of swords as they struggled vainly to keep the litter high in the air. The Spaniards turned the square and the surrounding plain into a killing field, and only their leader's intervention saved Atahualpa, as Pizarro roared above the din, "Let no one wound the Indian upon pain of death!" He then dragged Atahualpa into a building, there to be held under guard. Meanwhile, the massacre continued unabated. In the two hours before darkness fell, 6,000 Inca troops died in and around Cajamarca, yet not a single Spaniard was killed. Among the few to be wounded was Pizarro, slightly injured accidentally by one of his own men as he struggled to take his royal prisoner alive. "It was not accomplished by our own forces," one Spaniard commented afterward, "for there were so few of us. It was by the grace of God, which is great."

From that moment on, the Spaniards were the effective masters of the Inca empire, and nothing would ever be the same again. Commentators have since tried to understand why Atahualpa made the deadly error of marching unarmed into Cajamarca. Perhaps he was deceived by the blandishments of the Spaniards, who had spoken to him only of friendship and alliances. And when he heard from his spies that the bearded ones were huddling inside the buildings of the town, it probably suggested to him not ambush but cowardice.

Given the overwhelming numbers of his troops, Atahualpa had apparently not even considered the possibility that Pizarro's paltry force of fewer than 200 men would attempt to assault him, amid his vast army, in the heart of his empire. His lack of insight into

A POWERFUL FIGHTING FORCE WITH A BRONZE AGE ARSENAL

Because of the sheer manpower they could muster—often hundreds of thousands strong—and their impressive arsenal of short- and long-range weapons, the Incas had the most formidable armed force in South America, before the advent of the Spaniards.

MACE HEAD

Theirs was primarily a citizen army. All able-bodied men between the ages of 25 and 50 were subject to be drafted for up to five years. Each province supplied both rank and file and officers. At the bottom of the hierarchy, every 10 warriors formed a group, headed by a leader responsible for supplies and discipline. The next level of command was of five such groups, and two five-group units were placed under the dictate of a still-higher officer. Leadership thus rose in a pyra-

MACE WITH AX

mid to the commander in chief, the Sapa Inca.

This highly organized force was backed by an efficient communications and supply system. The Incas could move soldiers over thousands of miles of roads, dotted with storehouses stocked with food, clothing, and a variety of bronze weapons. Of these arms the sling, or *huaraca (below)*, was often the first employed, since fighting usually began at a distance. The soldier would slip an egg-sized stone into the middle of the fabric. After twirling the belt above his head, he would release one end, propelling the missile toward an opponent as far as 30 yards away.

Drawing closer, the warrior used a javelin. And in hand-to-hand combat, he might swing a rope, at the end of which flew a spiked copper mace *(upper left)* that he would

BOLA

slam into his foe's skull. Alternately, fighters employed star-shaped clubs, with copper, bronze, or stone heads fastened to wooden handles, sometimes with an ax blade attached *(center)*.

When the Spaniards invaded the Andes, their horses, swords, and firearms offered new targets. Adapting their tactics, the Incas relied more heavily on the bola *(upper right)*, three stones attached to lengths of llama tendons. The device was spun in the air and then launched toward the enemy. Entangling their legs, it brought mounts and men crashing to the ground.

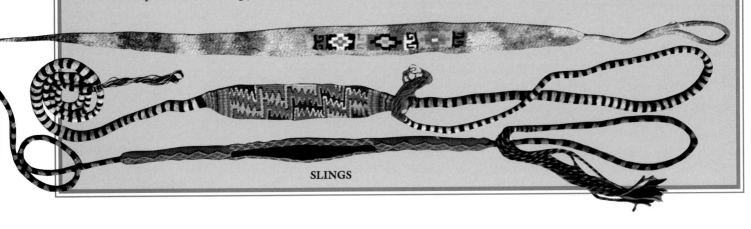

SLINGS

the invaders' mentality gave him no inkling of the confidence Pizarro and his men derived from their feeling of superiority to all peoples of the New World, whom they saw as heathens. They drew courage from the conviction that on their side was God, the powerful empire of Charles V, and the unrelenting forward thrust of European civilization. The Incas had harbored a similar faith in their destiny, but the smallpox epidemic and the civil war had done much to shake it.

On hearing of Atahualpa's capture and the massacre of so many of his troops, the general in charge, Rumiñavi, fled, with his men, north to Quito. The other two veteran generals were in Cuzco. Atahualpa himself was eager to keep his own forces at bay, fearing that the Spaniards would kill him if they were attacked by Incas.

In captivity, Atahualpa was allowed to maintain the trappings of a king. His women and servants lived in the closely guarded quarters assigned him, and his people still came to him for their orders, which were scrupulously obeyed. He knew, therefore, all that was happening within the empire and could transmit to his officials, when he wished, secret instructions. Within the space of 20 days, he learned to speak Spanish and also to read a little, an achievement that went beyond that of the illiterate Pizarro.

Shrewdly observing the glint that gold brought to the eyes of the bearded ones, Atahualpa resolved to buy them off by promising them history's most spectacular ransom. He agreed to fill the room in which he was being held—a chamber 22 feet long by 17 feet wide—with gold, piled up as far as he could reach above his head. He also said that he would fill a hut "twice over with silver."

When the Spaniards first heard Atahualpa's remarkable offer, they thought he was joking, but soon became convinced that his intentions were genuine. After Pizarro had a legal paper drawn up documenting this proposal, they sat back to wait while the treasure was brought to them. It began arriving by the llama-load—tumblers, vases, and finely wrought ornaments, including an idol the size of a

Of the vast amount of precious metalwork crafted in the Inca empire, only a few pieces remain, such as the 10-inch-long gold sculpture of seven seabirds shown above left. Almost all were melted down into ingots and shipped back to Spain to pay its mounting debt—and to be made into such extravagances as this gold-leaf altarpiece in the cathedral at Seville.

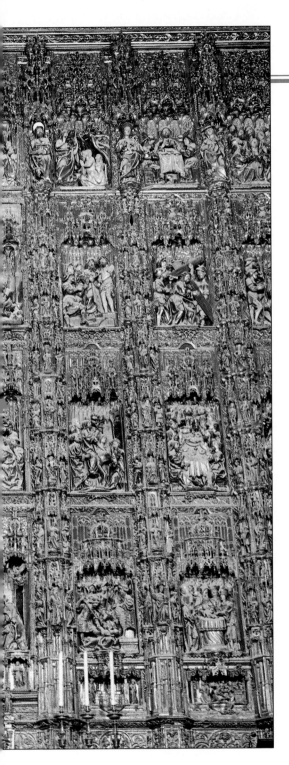

four-year-old child, as well as 700 plaques of gold stripped from the walls of temples in Cuzco, where they had been mounted over stone. These were thrown in pell-mell, along with delicately wrought models of plants and animals, even a fountain spouting a solid jet of gold with golden birds and animals playing in the pool below. One observer reported that he saw 200 loads of gold arrive from Cuzco, each on a litter supported by four bearers, while one litter was so weighed down with precious metal 12 people had to carry it.

Despite making good on his offer, Atahualpa had effectively signed his death warrant, again in a miscalculation of his adversaries. To the Incas, gold had little intrinsic worth. They called it the "sweat of the sun" (silver was the "tears of the moon") and saw the glittering metal as being aesthetically pleasing and hallowed, to be fashioned into beautiful objects or statues of gods to adorn holy places. They respected labor and put far more value on their extraordinary weavings, each cloth representing thousands of hours spent at the loom. These fabrics, rather than bullion, were the real currency of the empire. It was hardly likely, therefore, that Atahualpa could have comprehended the depth of European gold lust. Sending out orders to empty Cuzco of its treasures, he little imagined that nothing less than the entire wealth of the empire would satisfy the Spaniards. Atahualpa worried instead that the captive Huascar might offer the bearded ones an even larger amount of gold to purchase his own freedom. So he sent secret orders to his generals to kill his half brother, who perished with his wife and his mother; their bodies, it was said, were cut to pieces.

The last act of Atahualpa's tragedy was played out before the Spaniards left Cajamarca. Word of the empire's riches had filtered out of the country, attracting newcomers eager for a share of the loot. But to safeguard the treasure for themselves, Pizarro and his followers had agreed that the ransom would be divided up among them as the price for their courage, the lion's share going to the men who had been present at Atahualpa's capture. The gold alone, when melted down, came to 13,400 pounds, and the silver weighed even more—26,000 pounds. Since any booty seized while Atahualpa was still alive could be construed as part of the ransom, the late arrivals were eager to dispose of him in order to win their portion of future pickings. They spread the rumor that Atahualpa was plotting an assault by the Inca army to rescue him, which struck fear in the hearts of the outnumbered Spaniards. Atahualpa, realizing that a plot was afoot,

The foundations of one of three towers at the fortified temple of Sacsahuaman, scene of Inca resistance, reveal how it was constructed in triple stone circles. The outermost ring has a diameter of 75 feet.

HAUNTING RUINS OF INCA DEFEAT

In an attempt to regain control over their destiny, some 100,000 Incas besieged 190 Spaniards and their supporters within Cuzco in 1536. As part of their strategy, they hurled red-hot stones at the city's thatched roofs, setting them afire and nearly suffocating the enemy. Trapped, many of the desperate Spaniards asked their leaders to abandon the city, but a decision was made to fight back.

The Inca attacks on Cuzco came mainly from the massive hillside fortified temple of Sacsahuaman *(left)*. The Spaniards launched a 50-horse cavalry charge on the stronghold, withstanding showers of javelins and stone missiles lobbed from slingshots. By late afternoon, Juan Pizarro, Francisco's brother and the leader of the assault, received a mortal blow. The following day, the Inca ruler, Manco Inca, sent 5,000 reinforcements. The Spaniards then resorted to European siege tactics, scaling the walls and eventually driving the defenders into the fort's towers. Supplies there ran low. Still, resistance continued for several days more. Although the Spaniards had won Sacsahuaman, the Incas under Manco kept up their own siege of the city, which went on for a year. Perhaps because of the arrival of Spanish reinforcements or a lack of will on the part of his men, Manco retreated to the wild areas northwest of Cuzco to launch further resistance from there. But the Incas' fate had already been sealed.

now reconciled himself to death and shifted his attention to a noble objective—immortality. The Christian version held no meaning for him, but within his own religion the Sapa Inca was guaranteed life everlasting if his body was properly mummified, and to this end Atahualpa directed his final efforts.

Pizarro tried to restrain his men from taking hasty action against his prisoner, but eventually he was panicked into agreeing to the Inca's execution. Contemporary accounts record that there was no trial other than a meeting of Pizarro's council, who agreed that Atahualpa should be burned alive. He wept when told of his fate, for the destruction of his body would deny him immortality. "What have I or my children done to merit such a fate?" he asked Pizarro.

Tied to the stake, he listened while a friar made a last effort at conversion. Realizing that if he were baptized, he would be garroted rather than burned, he agreed to these rites, assuming that his body would be turned over to his people for mummification. In a final betrayal, after strangling him, the Spaniards burned part of his body and clothing. Then they buried him, as one grumbled, "with as much pomp as if he had been the most important Spaniard in our camp."

For all his suspicions of Atahualpa, Pizarro was not blind to the advantage of having a native ruler under Spanish control as a way of ensuring the obedience of the peoples of the far-flung empire. His choice, Manco Inca, a surviving son of Huayna Capac, who had supported Huascar against Atahualpa, was popular with the people of Cuzco, the stronghold of the Huascar faction. Still, these Cuzco residents took no chances; before the Spaniards entered their city, they took care to hide—not their gold but their most precious possessions, the mummies of former emperors. When Pizarro's men arrived, many welcomed them as restorers of the legitimate Inca line.

The Incas soon saw how mistaken they had been. When they had conquered neighboring peoples, they had normally allowed the local chiefs to retain their dignity as well as their titles so long as they agreed to rule alongside the Inca governors. But the conquistadors proved much less generous. They abused Manco and showed no regard for Inca customs. Worse

In fierce defiance of their conquerors, traditionally armed Inca warriors battle Spanish soldiers. Inca resistance, depicted on this wooden kero from postconquest Peru, continued from 1532 until 1572 when Viceroy Toledo called for the use of "fire and blood" against the Inca empire's last stronghold, Vilcabamba.

was to come when Pizarro quit Cuzco for the coast to found a new capital, Lima. He left his younger brother, Gonzalo, in charge, with another brother, Juan, to assist him. Gonzalo treated Manco with undisguised contempt, even abducting and raping his favorite wife.

With reports of Spanish atrocities flooding in from around the empire, the previously pliable Manco balked at further compliance. He attempted to escape from Cuzco, but was captured and brought back in chains. Placed in jail, he was subjected to further humiliations by his captors, who, he later claimed, urinated on him and burned his eyelashes with candles. From that time on there was no longer any question of accommodation with the Spaniards.

Soon after Gonzalo departed on a mission of reprisal for the murder of several of his countrymen, Manco persuaded Hernando Pizarro, another of Francisco's brothers, who had recently come to Cuzco from Spain, to release him so that he might pray at a shrine where there was a golden effigy of his father. He said that he wanted to present the statue to Hernando as a gift, and apparently the Spaniard believed him. Once out of Cuzco, Manco called on his people to revolt. At last they had a champion to lead them against the invaders, and, in the tens of thousands, they flocked to join him. In a moment of triumph that validated the Inca organizational genius, warriors were recruited, fed, and transported to the outskirts of Cuzco, without alerting the Spaniards to their movements. Alarming news reached Francisco Pizarro in his new city: Cuzco was under siege.

The siege was to last for almost a year, during which the Inca capital was effectively cut off from the rest of the country. A fierce, two-week battle for control of the fortresslike temple of Sacsahuaman was won by the Spaniards. During the siege Indian collaborators in and around Cuzco had sneaked food to the Spaniards. These traitors included some of Manco's own relatives, who, like others, feared retaliation for their earlier support of the Europeans if Manco gained the upper hand. The siege failed when Spanish reinforcements arrived. Manco's followers saw that their best opportunity was gone, and most drifted away.

The results of the conquest for the peoples of the Inca empire were terrible indeed. The shock of defeat was more than they could bear, and many lost their will to live as the empire deteriorated all around them. Estimates suggest that the population of Tahuantinsuyu may have been reduced by three-quarters in the half-century after the arrival of the Spaniards, from perhaps seven million to about

500,000. On those who were not carried off by smallpox and by measles, which had also been introduced by the Europeans, enforced labor took a further toll. Coast dwellers expired of exhaustion and cold when they were made to carry heavy loads into the high mountains, and others died working in gold and silver mines.

All aspects of native culture came under European attack. Palaces were desecrated, and the sun temples destroyed. The royal mummies were found and burned. Most of the masterworks of Inca gold- and silversmiths were transformed into ingots. Some of the most beautiful objects were sent to Europe as a present for Charles V. There they were exhibited in Seville, to the wonder of all who saw them. Then, in an egregious act of vandalism, the emperor, short of cash for his military campaigns, ordered them melted down.

A remnant of the Incas chose to continue the struggle. After the failure of the siege of Cuzco, Manco led 20,000 supporters into a remote jungle area. There he and his followers created, in short order, the city Bingham had searched for. Graced with 60 monumental stone buildings and 300 smaller ones and crisscrossed by roads and canals, Vilcabamba spread out over two square miles. The Incas would reign here for another three and a half decades. From their forested fastness, they occasionally struck out at the empire's conquerors, waging guerrilla warfare against Spanish outposts. After Manco's death, three of his sons, in succession, ruled Vilcabamba.

In 1572, the Spaniards decided to eliminate this last vestige of native hegemony. Reaching Vilcabamba, they found it nearly deserted; its defenders had fired the city to deny it to their victors before taking flight. But the Spaniards continued their pursuit deep into the rain forest, and there the last Inca leader, Tupac Amaru, fell into their hands. He was taken back to Cuzco, subjected to a show trial, and beheaded in the town square. With him ended the Inca dynasty.

Silence fell over Vilcabamba. The jungle returned, hiding the city's temples and palaces under a cloak of vegetation, with a mere hint of past habitation left only in the name Spanish-speaking peasants later gave to the valley area—Espíritu Pampa, Plain of Ghosts. Since Hiram Bingham's journey of 1911, archaeologists and explorers have returned to Vilcabamba several times, peaceful invaders seeking to wrest the last secrets of the Inca from the vegetation's grip. Much has been discovered, but no one can say that the concealing jungle has yielded up all the city's secrets, or that the full story of the Incas' last days has been fully told.

MACHU PICCHU REVEALED

Something hidden!" wrote Rudyard Kipling. "Go and find it! Go and look behind the ranges—something lost behind the ranges. Lost and waiting for you. Go!" And Hiram Bingham, the American explorer, went, inspired by the English poet's verse to search out Peru's hidden wonders. His discoveries were numerous, but none caught the world's imagination more than his finding of Machu Picchu.

Theories of Machu Picchu's past abound. Bingham himself ardently—but erroneously—claimed the mountaintop settlement to be Tambo-toco, the mythic birthplace of the first Inca, as well as Vilcabamba, the Incas' last stronghold.

Although its protected location suggests a citadel, Machu Picchu lacks serious man-made defenses. Indeed, the quality of the stonework and the number of buildings of religious significance led scholars to conclude that the town was erected as a sacred retreat by the great ruler Pachacuti a century before the conquest.

Hardly large enough to be a city, Machu Picchu contains fewer than 200 buildings—temples, residences, structures for storage and other public uses—most built of well-cut, tight-fitting stone. It is thought that up to 1,200 residents may have lived here and in the outlying areas, worshiping the sun god, Inti, and farming agricultural terraces.

Until Hiram Bingham wandered awe-stricken through the overgrown ruins on July 24, 1911, accompanied by a government-appointed escort and a local boy, few outsiders had set foot in Machu Picchu since its mysterious desertion, sometime after 1532—and before the Spaniards began their push inland. The photographs Bingham shot that day, the basis of this essay, show the neglect of centuries. In them, Machu Picchu seems not unlike a fairy-tale castle sleeping away the years, untouched in its bramble cocoon. Now cleared and excavated, the ruins present a far different but no less imposing spectacle.

HIDDEN CITY IN THE CLOUDS

Inaccessible and unmapped, Machu Picchu was still never a lost city in the true sense, although Hiram Bingham deserves credit for its discovery. Indeed, when he arrived at the site, he found farmers who had taken up residence, "free from undesirable visitors, officials looking for army 'volunteers' or collecting taxes," as they confided to him. In addition, a few sightseers had passed through—leaving their names charcoaled over the granite walls.

The blackened tree trunks in Bingham's photograph at left indicate where the farmers had burned jungle growth to clear some of the terraces, which they described as being suitable for growing corn, potatoes, sugarcane, beans, peppers, tamarillos, and gooseberries. The exuberance of the wild foliage presented a frustrating challenge to Bingham and early excavators attempting to clear the site. Removing the graffiti from the fine granite required extra days' labor as well—a vexing waste of precious time for Bingham, who chafed under the irony that Peruvian authorities had warned his team not to "deface or mutilate" the ruins in any way.

Majestic Huayna Picchu rises behind a group of structures peering through tangled foliage on the eastern edge of the city looking west. Hiram Bingham's 1911 photograph—actually two of his shots spliced together—is the first view of Machu Picchu ever captured on film.

A STURDY TOWER FOR WORSHIPING THE SUN

At the southeastern end of Machu Picchu, Inca masons erected two imposing structures, a semicircular tower and a multilevel adjacent building, both of which Bingham regarded as the "work of a master artist." The tower's resemblance to a curving section of the Temple of the Sun in Cuzco induced him to attach the same name to this find.

Because the tower and its associated edifices evoke a medieval fortress, Peruvians later dubbed the complex El Torreón, "the bastion," but its purpose was certainly religious, as Bingham sensed. The tower was constructed around an upthrusted piece of living rock carved to serve as an altar. Beneath the tower, out of sight in both Bingham's photo at left and a recent shot of the area *(below)*, lies a grotto *(page 75)* that Bingham thought may have housed the mummies of Inca rulers, although scholars now think it more likely that it functioned as a ritual chamber. The building in the foreground of the shots captivated Bingham with its mortarless, perfectly fitted granite walls; in his view, their craftsmanship was "as fine as the finest stonework in the world." He theorized that the *mamaconas*—beautiful, holy "chosen women" who wove garments, prepared meals, and brewed alcoholic *chicha* for priests and nobility—resided in this temple complex.

"A wonderful effect, softer and more pleasing than that of the marble temples of the Old World," wrote Bingham of the granite wall in his photograph at left. Part of the so-called House of the Princess, the wall joins with El Torreón (rear), the semicircular structure that he reverently named the Temple of the Sun.

Now excavated, the complex exhibits the beauty and precision it possessed more than four centuries ago. A stairway in front of the House of the Princess leads to the tower, from which a trapezoidal window affords a view of the valley below. The opening may have been used by priests to monitor the sun's path around the time of the winter solstice.

THE SACRED PLAZA AND ITS WONDERS

"Surprise followed surprise in bewildering succession," marveled Bingham as he surveyed the Sacred Plaza, thought to have been Machu Picchu's religious center. On the north side of a clearing stood a three-sided edifice of white granite that "contained blocks of Cyclopean size, higher than a man." Extending from the western wall of the temple, a small enclosure called the Ornament Chamber offered vivid testimony to the stonemasons' brilliance: Two of its enormous foundation blocks are each carved with 32 corners in three dimensions, fitting snugly with the adjacent stones. "The sight held me spellbound," Bingham exclaimed.

Perhaps the most provocative of Machu Picchu's buildings is the three-sided temple on the eastern edge of the plaza, featuring a trio of large trapezoidal windows open to the rising sun, flanked by blind windows of equal size that may have served as niches. According to a native chronicle, the first Inca ruler ordered a temple built at his birthplace of Tambo-toco, with three windows to symbolize caves, "the home of his fathers from whom he was descended." Bingham thought this might be the very spot. Unfortunately, the enticing speculation crumbled before evidence that Machu Picchu's architectural style is late Inca.

In a modern view, the Temple of the Three Windows has been partly restored to reflect its once-pristine glory. The single stone at the center of the open side probably helped support a roof. The granite slab in the foreground may have been a sacred stone, or merely part of a collapsed wall. To the left of the Temple of the Three Windows, a portion of the city's principal temple is visible.

Believing that human figures added interest and scale to his photographs, Bingham posed his escort, Sergeant Carrasco, on the massive Temple of the Three Windows (below). He worked meticulously, using slow shutter speeds to achieve crisp images filled with minute detail.

HITCHING POST OF THE SUN

Winding away from the Sacred Plaza and up a terraced granite outcrop, a long stairway charts a dramatic climb to a carved, polygonal stone at the summit—the *intihuatana,* or "hitching post of the sun," in its colorful translation. (*Inti* means sun; *huata,* to tie.) Here, Bingham hypothesized, the Incas may have symbolically tethered the sun to prevent it from straying away at the winter solstice. "The priests," he wrote, "able, on the twenty-first or twenty-second of June, to stop its flight and tie it to a stone pillar in one of their temples, were regarded with veneration."

The elegant stone, sculpted from the mountain itself, may have served as a solar observatory, allowing priests to determine the best times for sowing and harvesting crops by noting the disappearance of its shadow at the spring and fall equinoxes. On these occasions, the priests would have decked the stone with great quantities of flowers and herbs. In particular, during the Inti Raymi—the magnificent sun festivals held in June and December—the residents of Machu Picchu probably gathered at the intihuatana for days of harmonious chanting, effigy rituals, and prayers.

Jutting almost six feet from the ground, the monumental intihuatana—carved from the granite bedrock—is the tallest Inca monument of its kind still in existence. Apparently the Inca sculptor cut away only those portions of the stone that did not possess huaca, or holy aspect.

Surrounded by jungle growth, Bingham's escort, Sergeant Carrasco, places his hand on the stone, the so-called intihuatana, most likely used by the Incas for worship of the sun god, Inti. Beside him stands the anonymous farmer's son who guided Bingham and Carrasco into the ruins.

Spreading over the Andean spine, the excavated terraces and granite buildings of Machu Picchu resemble a "patterned blanket thrown over a great rock," in the words of Yale University art historian George Kubler. The city's beauty lies in its remarkable integration of architecture and environment.

AN EMPIRE BUILT BY A MAN CALLED EARTHSHAKER

Found near the body of a boy who was probably sacrificed to the sun god, this silver figurine clad in parrot feathers and luxurious vicuna wool may represent a deity intended as the child's escort into the next world.

Taking advantage of a pleasant Sunday afternoon in May 1950, about a third of Cuzco's residents, some 15,000 people, had flocked to the outskirts of the Peruvian town for a soccer match. Others had gone to church, or were strolling the cobbled streets, when, in a sudden lacerating shudder, an earthquake ripped apart the city, toppling buildings and leaving 83 people dead beneath the debris. Although the cataclysm shook the city for only seconds, its political tremors continued to ripple through Cuzco's social structure for six years as the 400-year-old domination of the Indian past by Spanish culture was dislodged.

Many of the buildings erected by the Spaniards on the ruins of the Inca capital collapsed under the earthquake's impact, and the narrow old streets were strewn with granite blocks that to one witness looked like nothing so much as "big black dice." As in earlier quakes, however, most of the oldest stone foundations of Cuzco withstood the fierce seismic blows. These were the finely crafted walls that the Incas had painstakingly fitted together without benefit of mortar, five centuries before, in creating what the conquistador Pedro Sancho conceded was a city "so large and so beautiful that it would be remarkable even in Spain."

Near the center of Cuzco, under the rubble of the 16th-century church of Santo Domingo and a portion of its monastery, a magnificent 20-foot-high curved retaining wall of dark gray andesite remained intact, as did the complex's other Inca stonework. And to the wonder and delight of many, the earthquake had laid bare additional stretches of imposing Inca walls previously hidden by the colonial structures.

These splendid walls, upon which Dominican friars had first built their church and monastery, once belonged to the holiest shrine in the Inca empire: the Temple of the Sun, dedicated to Inti, the supreme deity. The Incas called this compound of a half-dozen buildings the Coricancha, the "golden enclosure." Here, alongside an effigy of Inti himself, they had placed the idols of the peoples they had subjugated. Daily rituals honoring the god were performed in the main temple—and in other temples modeled on the Coricancha throughout the realm—by the high priests and the cloistered women whom the Spaniards had memorably dubbed Virgins of the Sun. At the break of each day, Inti's devotees threw to the rising sun a ceremonial kiss, known as the *mocha*.

The Spaniards were dazzled by the Coricancha. The chronicler Pedro de Cieza de León declared Inti's temple to be "among the richest in gold and silver to be found anywhere in the world." He described how "halfway up the wall ran a stripe of gold two handspans wide and four fingers thick. The gateway and doors were covered with sheets of this metal. There was an image of the sun, of great size, made of gold, beautifully wrought and set with many precious stones. There was a garden in which the earth was lumps of fine gold, and it was cunningly planted with stalks of corn that were of gold—stalk, leaves, and ears."

A bountiful harvest of gold and silver from the Coricancha helped pay Atahualpa's ransom after he was taken prisoner by the conquistadors. The Spaniards stripped 700 gold plates from the walls alone—"like boards from chests," noted Pizarro's secretary. When melted down, each plaque yielded an ingot of four and a half pounds. Having plundered its riches, the conquerors turned the shell of the Coricancha over to the Dominicans, the powerful religious order that had administered the brutal Spanish Inquisition.

Even in its denuded state the Coricancha was impressive, and though much altered over the centuries, it became a lure to scholars probing its secrets. In the late 19th century, the friars permitted the American diplomat and archaeologist Ephraim George Squier to, as he said, "ransack every portion of the church, and every nook and

corner of the convent, and to measure and sketch and photograph to my fill. Here a long reach of massive wall, yonder a fragment, now a corner, next a doorway, and anon a terrace—through the aid of these I was able to make up a ground plan of the ancient edifice." In 1928, the German archaeologist Max Uhle discovered previously hidden remnants of the original Inca structure beneath a side altar. Then, in the 1940s, the archaeologist John H. Rowe of the University of California pored over the monastery and mapped out a general floor plan, which was largely validated when hidden portions of the Inca structures came to light in 1950.

Earthquakes had forced the Dominicans to rebuild their church several times over the centuries. But after the extensive damage of 1950, an unprecedented public outcry on behalf of the older structures compelled restorers to grapple with a dilemma their predecessors had not faced: Which ruins should be saved—the Spanish colonial church or the Inca temple? A team of advisers sent to Cuzco in 1951 by UNESCO (United Nations Educational, Scientific, and Cultural Organization) resisted local pleas in favor of the temple and recommended restoration of the church, citing its value as a beautiful and important example of early colonial architecture. But public pressure mounted to preserve the monuments of Peru's Inca civilization at the expense of its Spanish heritage. By the time Peruvian architects began serious restoration six years later, planners had decided to ignore UNESCO's recommendation and give priority

Symbolizing the clash of two cultures, the reconstructed Spanish church of Santo Domingo sits atop its Inca foundation, the curved wall of the Temple of the Sun, at Cuzco. Built during the reign of Pachacuti from perfectly fitted blocks of dark igneous rock, the sacred wall of the Coricancha—"golden enclosure"—has withstood centuries of earthquakes, while the colonial structure above it has crumbled and been repaired many times over.

49

to the Inca ruins. Since then, several sections of the church and monastery have been removed to reveal part of the labyrinth of walls once sheathed in gold, revered by the Incas as the "sweat of the sun."

    It was only fitting that this small triumph on behalf of the vanquished Incas should have occurred in Cuzco. Lodged in a valley on the western slopes of the snowcapped Andes 11,000 feet above sea level, the city had been the political, religious, and ceremonial core of the Inca world, possessing, according to the chronicler Cieza de León, an "air of nobility." Cuzco began humbly, one of several small farmers' villages in the valley, and perhaps would have languished as such had not the hero Inca Yupanqui risen to power there less than a century before the Spanish conquest. Possessed by a vision of Inca supremacy, this skillful military man and brilliant political organizer managed, in scarcely more than three decades, to expand his little domain into Tahuantinsuyu, "land of the four quarters," a realm that in its size and efficiency rivaled the Roman Empire at its height. The royal name he chose for himself was, appropriately enough, Pachacuti—which means cataclysm or earthshaker.

Under Pachacuti, perhaps the greatest leader produced in ancient America, and his son, Topa Inca Yupanqui, the Incas subdued every major state and tribe in the Andean region, thus creating not only the largest empire in the pre-Columbian New World but also the most carefully planned and administered one. They applied their remarkable organizational ability with a fervor that captivated the Spanish conquerors almost as much as did their gold. Indeed, so effective were they that, like the old walls of Cuzco, many of their ideas and practices survive today among the populations of the countries their empire once encompassed.

Because the Incas lacked writing and could not set down in words their formidable accomplishments, they present modern scholars with the difficult problem of sorting fact from legend. Much of what is known about the earliest Incas has come from stories passed from one generation to another by the people. European travelers and missionaries often blended the tales they heard into their descriptions of the empire. Thus the surviving record is a colorful mix of truth and legend, tinged, in some instances, by Inca propaganda.

Still in its infancy, Peruvian archaeology has been struggling both to correct the ambiguities and misinterpretations and to verify the accuracy of the old accounts. Considered one of the most reliable of the Spanish chroniclers is Pedro de Cieza de León, who for 17 years roamed about the empire as a common soldier. Though he viewed the Incas through the lens of a different culture—and that of a conqueror to boot—he proved a careful listener and a keen observer. Another important chronicler, El Inca Garcilaso de la Vega, was the son of an Inca princess and a Spanish soldier; he knew the

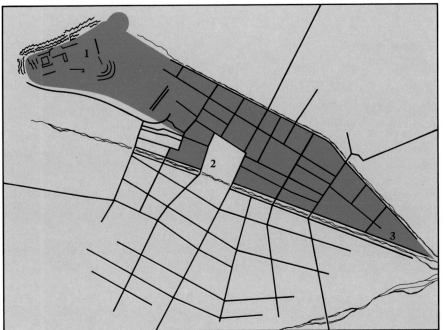

As illustrated in the diagram above, the ancient Inca capital of Cuzco was designed in the shape of a puma, holy symbol of strength and power; the outline is still visible at the heart of the modern-day city (opposite). Ramparts at the puma's head (1) held the fortified temple complex of Sacsahuaman; royal palaces and administrative and religious buildings surrounded a huge plaza set in the puma's midsection (2); and noble families made their homes in the Puma Chupan, or puma's tail (3), an area located at the point where two rivers that had been turned into canals flow together.

indigenous customs and language. But his status as a half-caste held in inferior regard by the Spaniards led him to extol, on occasion, the virtues of his mother's heritage at the expense of the truth.

As far as can be determined from the patchy historical record, the Incas date back to about AD 1200. That much is known from a chronological list of their rulers. They descended from a small ethnic group of highlanders living in the Cuzco valley, but the details of their early existence soon fade into myth. The word *Inca* did not even appear in the Incas' own oral histories until mention of the sixth ruler, who adopted the title Sapa Inca. Only later did these mountain dwellers themselves come to be known as Incas.

According to the legends still learned by Peruvian schoolchildren, the founder of Cuzco was Manco Capac, the first ruler. He and his people, as one myth has it, emerged from one of three caves at Paccaritambo, 18 miles to the southwest. Other myths have Manco appearing on an island in Lake Titicaca, much farther to the south. At Cuzco, say the legends, Manco plunged a golden staff into the ground where the glittering Coricancha would rise. The fertile earth swallowed the rod, thus signifying its acceptance.

The ancient stories establish the Incas as the children of the sun god, Inti, who entrusted·them with the task of taming and educating the savages they encountered. But however blessed they may have been, their ascent to greatness was slow, in part because they gained supremacy initially through intermarriage with other groups in the Cuzco valley. Over the course of two centuries, the Incas managed to subdue some of their neighbors, expanding their realm within the perimeter of a dozen or so miles around Cuzco.

The Incas did not begin to fulfill their true destiny until the emergence of their ninth ruler, Pachacuti. He could not have had a more inauspicious start as a young man: He was just one of the many sons of the eighth ruler; indeed, his brother, Urcon, had already been named successor by their father. Pachacuti might have languished in the background had he not been called to his life's work by Inti in a vision, which, if nothing else, suggests the vast scope of the prince's early ambition. According to a story told to Father Bernabé Cobo, a 17th-century Jesuit missionary, Inti appeared to Pachacuti with snakes coiling around his arms. "Upon seeing this image," recounted Cobo, "Pachacuti became so terrified that he started to flee." The sun god reassured him: "Come here, my child, have no fear, for I am your father the sun. I know that you will subjugate many nations and take great care to honor me and remember me in your sacrifices."

Inti then revealed to him by means of a magic crystal images of all the regions Pachacuti would conquer. But it took a military crisis to give the young prince the opportunity he needed. In 1438, Cuzco came under threat of attack by a powerful force of warriors known as the Chancas. The danger was so great that Pachacuti's aging father, Viracocha Inca, and Urcon, the heir apparent, fled to a mountain fortress, taking along with them their best soldiers.

Whether powered by his vision or goaded by a desire to show up Urcon—or both—Pachacuti refused to leave. As the Chancas prepared to storm Cuzco, he took charge. To augment his own few troops, he drew men from neighboring tribes. When the Chancas opened their assault at dawn, Pachacuti was ready. Clad in the skin of a puma, an animal that the Incas regarded as the embodiment of strength and power, he led the counterattack. At the critical moment, say the legends, he summoned supernatural aid. The very stones on the battlefield turned into warriors, and their ghostly ranks helped repel the enemy. Cuzco was safe.

Pachacuti now forced his father to abdicate and took the throne. He then went on to a series of other military triumphs. With an army composed of men from other conquered tribes but officered solely by Incas, he gradually extended his dominion north into the central Peruvian highlands and then south to the shores of Lake Titicaca. As the Spanish-Inca chronicler Garcilaso put it, "A prince's thirst for conquest, like his ambition, increases with his power."

But Pachacuti had a vision of the future. Warfare in the past had been largely a matter of looting and then withdrawing to the home territory. He used war differently—not just to acquire diverse resources but also to spread Inca culture and religion. He knew that the Incas were regarded by their enemies as formidable foes. They traditionally embarked upon new campaigns singing the grisly victory song that, too often, became literal truth: "From his skull we shall drink. We shall adorn ourselves with his teeth. His bones will serve as our flutes. With his skin for a drum, we shall dance." Yet Pachacuti also knew that, to achieve victory, it might suffice merely to strike terror in his enemies, rather than to actually engage them in combat. He would send emissaries to a foe preaching the advantages of surrender. Spanish chronicles tell how he would invite his adversaries "in the name of the Sun to acknowledge his authority, upon which they would be treated with honor and loaded with presents." Not surprisingly, the promise of peace and gifts, backed by the threat of slaughter, often had the desired effect—capitulation without struggle.

While the Incas were not the first Indians to build an Andean empire, they could, thanks to the expansion of their territory by Pachacuti and his heir, Topa Inca Yupanqui, lay claim to the largest domain, and the most ecologically diverse. Anyone who crosses the territories their empire encompassed will be amazed by its geographical extremes. A traveler starting on the coast near present-day Lima, and moving east across the mountains, passes through a bewildering succession of landscapes and environments. He begins a few feet above sea level, in one of the driest deserts on earth. Climbing into the hills behind the city, he rapidly mounts the first Andes range; at Ticlo Pass, 66 miles inland, he has reached 16,000 feet—higher than any summit in the American Rockies. From there he drops thousands of feet to the bleak, open grasslands of the puna, and on down to the 10,000-foot-high valley of the Mantaro River. And his trip has just begun. He must now cross the snowfields of the White Cordillera, 16,500 feet up, then descend through the mist-shrouded forests of the *montaña* to the Apurimac canyon, only a few thousand feet above sea level. Veering southeast, he reaches the high ridges of the Vilcabamba range, and then enters the jungles of the Urubamba region. He has traveled less than 300 miles as the condor flies, from almost sea level into the clouds, through wildly differing ecological realms, and along brinks of mountain gorges that plunge to abysses below. And he has still not experienced the full dimension of the Incas' realm.

Massive stone terraces served as agricultural platforms for the temple citadel at Ollantaytambo, a mountaintop retreat about 45 miles northwest of Cuzco. Blocks of polished pink stone, apparently intended for a building project that was never completed, dot the rocky spur that towers over the site, below which lay a royal estate planned out by Pachacuti.

Traveling in the mountains places severe strains on the human body. Lack of oxygen at these altitudes causes nausea and headache, turning each breath into a labored gasp. Skin cracks in the dry air, and toes and fingers stiffen in the cold. With time the body adapts; to ease the stress, the Incas chewed coca—an energizing narcotic leaf that grows in the montaña.

It seems extraordinary that any people could survive at such extremes, much less build a great civilization. Beyond the hardships of high-altitude living is the dangerous instability of the land itself. The Andes are young mountains on the scale of geologic time, subject to adolescent turmoil. One or another of dozens of volcanoes periodically spews forth its fiery contents. Earthquakes rumble through the highlands, sending mud slides and avalanches into the valleys below. One avalanche in 1970 snuffed out 20,000 lives, burying an entire city.

Then there is the problem of rainfall. The coast is so dry along most of its expanse that annual precipitation is too slight to measure. Nothing will grow unless artificially watered. Only in the high cordillera, above 10,000 feet, does rain fall in appreciable quantities. Its arrival is seasonal. In winter, the land remains arid; but come spring, moisture-laden easterlies gust up from the Amazon basin, and cloud banks darken the mountain crests. Rain pours down on the eastern montaña, 90 inches a year in places, while hailstorms and blizzards buffet the higher ridges.

With a domain so vast and far-flung, the Incas needed the kinds of systems that would enable them to govern effectively. Scattered throughout the extremes of this challenging geography were different ethnic groups with little in common. After conquering them, Pachacuti faced the task of orchestrating them into a single burgeoning empire. Not all of history's conquerors have had the desire or the talent for governance, but Pachacuti wanted to devote full time to ruling his newly acquired lands, so he turned over the army to his son Topa Inca in 1463. In the succeeding years, Pachacuti invented ingenious mechanisms for governing and borrowed others from the Andean societies his army subdued.

Once Pachacuti had seized a new territory, he set sound policy calculated to prevent unrest. For example, he allowed conquered peoples to keep their leaders and gods, although he did expect them to add worship of the sun god to their regular ritual. Unlike the Spaniards, who insisted on promulgating their religion to the exclusion of others, he welcomed local idols into the Inca pantheon, granting them a place in the revered Coricancha—which was his way actually of holding them hostage. If any unrest were indeed to arise in the lands from which they came, he could always order the revered effigies removed and publicly scourged, an act of such potential disgrace to those who adored the gods that they would have no choice but to knuckle under.

So that everyone in his empire could understand and communicate with one another, Pachacuti made Quechua, spoken in Cuzco, the official language. He allowed people still to speak their native tongues, of which the most widespread was Aymara, but they were required to learn Quechua. Cieza de León writes that "this was so strictly enforced that an infant had not yet left its mother's breast before they began to teach it the language it had to know." He described it as "a very good tongue, succinct, easily grasped, and rich in words." Its vocabulary includes the word equivalents of the phrases *well spoken* and *poorly spoken,* indicating a respect for the niceties of speech. Quechua survives today, used by an estimated 10 million Andean peoples, and Aymara lives on in some areas as well.

Pachacuti went to enormous lengths to justify the Inca empire's legitimacy. A master propagandist, he reportedly summoned his historians and dictated to them a new self-enhancing history to supersede all the older legends. One of its stories concerns a young woman in the dry coastal region of Ica, who allegedly repulsed Pachacuti's advances because she loved another man. Instead of being angry, Pachacuti admired her constancy and offered to reward her. Wishing nothing for herself, she asked for water for her village. The Sapa Inca then ordered 40,000 soldiers to dig the canals that would bring the liquid to the parched area. Through this story Pachacuti entered popular consciousness as the benevolent father of irrigation; it did not seem to matter that this extraordinary engineering feat had, in fact, been carried out at Ica centuries before his reign.

When his blandishments did not have their desired effect and the rebellion of subjects seemed more than a possibility, Pachacuti could always fall back on the threat of resettlement. During his reign, troublesome elements—on occasion, entire ethnic groups—were uprooted and dispatched to another part of the empire to meld into already-established provinces. They were replaced by people loyal to

Pachacuti, imported to set an example and to propagate Inca ways. Such resettlement also served three other useful purposes: It relieved pressure on densely populated areas by siphoning off the excess population, opened up virgin land to farming by making a pioneering work force available, and provided manpower for special projects. But its principal effect was to turn the empire into an enormous melting pot that could be stirred only from Cuzco.

Hierarchy, with the Sapa Inca set firmly at the pinnacle, was the dominant organizing principle of Inca government. Pachacuti asserted that, as a descendant of the sun god, he ruled by divine right. Opulence and reverence surrounded his person. While details of his daily life do not survive, a description by Cieza de León of the rituals surrounding another monarch, Atahualpa, gives some idea of how he must have been treated. In all likelihood his food, served in dishes of gold and silver, would have been brought to him and laid upon a mat at his feet. In Atahualpa's case, a woman attendant would hold each of his dishes as he ate; another would extend her hands to catch his spit if he had to clear his throat. Atahualpa's person was considered so sacred that his leftover food and clothing—discarded after being worn once—was saved and ceremonially burned at year's end.

When Pachacuti traveled to inspect his empire, he did not walk as a mortal but was conveyed in a golden litter encrusted with jewels, accompanied by an entourage that could number in the thousands. He held audiences—generally concealed behind a wall—seated upon a low stool that stood on a raised platform, a kind of throne and judgment seat combined, and wore a many-colored crown known as the *llautu,* a braid the width of a finger wound four or five times around the forehead. While the nobility could also wear a llautu, the emperor's was topped with three feathers and was draped in front with a distinctive fringe of red vicuña wool tassels that hung above his eyes and were attached to gold tubes. No one ever stood in the immediate presence of the ruler facing him, but turned his head and shoulders away. Even a noble approached the Sapa Inca with humility, barefoot, with a burden attached to his back. "It did not matter whether this weight was large or small," noted Cieza de León, "for it was only a token of the reverence due to the Inca."

As Sapa Inca, Pachacuti inherited the customs of his predecessors, some of which he modified to take into account the ever-

57

growing status of his position at the head of an expanding empire. Traditionally, the ruler was allowed a harem of hundreds of concubines, who served him as secondary wives. The empress, or Coya, however, came from the ranks of the Sapa Inca's full sisters. Being of royal blood and an heiress of the Sapa Inca in her own right, the Coya validated her husband's claim to the throne.

From the Coya's offspring, the emperor selected his heir. He chose on the basis of perceived competence, sometimes changing his mind later. The problem with this mode of succession was demonstrated when Pachacuti's grandson, Huayna Capac, died, apparently of smallpox, before officially designating his heir. His most likely successor, Ninan Cuyuchi, also died in the smallpox epidemic that swept the court, leaving two surviving princes, Huascar and Atahualpa, to fight it out between themselves as to who should have the crown. Thus started the civil war that preceded the downfall of the empire.

The Coya had her own court—and a reputation for taking an unofficial but discreet role in imperial affairs. She was often referred to affectionately by her subjects as Mamanchic—"our mother." An outstanding Coya, the wife of the fourth emperor, Mayta Capac, supposedly not only managed the female workers on the royal estates but also pursued investigations into the natural sciences. She introduced new plants for cultivation, encouraged the art of fishing, and even experimented with extracting poisons from snakes to render arrowheads more lethal.

At the top of a three-tiered structure of nobility, the hereditary aristocracy constituted the only caste that could truly be called Incas. Known as Capac Incas, they were the descendants of the legendary founder of the Inca dynasty, Manco Capac. They controlled all of the land as well as the distribution of the empire's most prized resources, including its llamas, alpacas, and vicunas; gold and silver, coca leaves, artifacts created by the finest artisans, and the most beautiful women in

The gold statuette at left exhibits the typical hairstyle of Inca women: long and parted in the middle. Women of status donned tapestry-weave gowns and shawls fastened with an ornamental pin, or tupu *(above). Noblemen wore ear spools like those adorning the silver figurine at right, plus a cloak and tunic, a headdress, and a bag for coca (above, right).*

the realm. They dressed in knee-length tunics woven of soft vicuna wool, a cloth forbidden to commoners. In the great palaces of Inca cities, their apartments might be adorned with fine tapestries, and the window frames sometimes plated with silver. Wives of aristocrats wore long, floor-length tunics, gathered at the waist by a sash bearing heraldic devices, and mantles fastened with ornate gold, silver, or bronze pins, known as *tupu* pins. Devoting hours every day to their personal appearance, they bathed regularly and kept their black uncut hair always clean, well combed, and shining. An Inca noblewoman held a claim in her own right to Andean resources, including a share of the labor and tribute of the peasantry. The system of inheritance according them these privileges, independent of their husband's status, has been termed parallel descent by one scholar, meaning that the male inherits from his father, the female through her mother.

The highest positions in the bureaucracy, army, and priesthood were held by adult noblemen, who probably never numbered more than five hundred. From among their restricted ranks were chosen the four top-ranking prefects, or *apus,* who governed each of Tahuantinsuyu's quarters and the many provinces into which each quarter was subdivided. As Pachacuti expanded the empire, one flaw in this arrangement soon became apparent: There were not enough qualified nobles to send to the new territories to safeguard and manage Inca interests and to inspire the people with their own good example. Ever the pragmatist, Pachacuti solved the problem by creating a new tier of Incas by royal decree. These appointed nobles were called Hahua Incas, meaning Incas by privilege or by adoption. Often they were leaders from around the Cuzco area whose loyalty Pachacuti knew to be strong, but many Indians of humbler origins who had performed a valuable service for the Sapa Inca were also vaulted into the ranks of the Hahua Incas.

Whether born or not to their title, all male Incas of privilege wore large honorary gold or silver disks that stretched their earlobes and caused the Spaniards to refer to them as *orejones—* "big ears." Wearing the earplugs was so prestigious an honor that such Incas looked upon a comrade who had suffered a torn ear in battle as truly unfortunate because he would now no longer be able to display the emblem of his elite status.

59

THE WEAVER'S ART: GOODS MORE PRECIOUS THAN GOLD

To the invading Spaniards, gold was without question the great prize in the Inca empire. But among the Incas themselves, textiles ranked as the most treasured commodity, in large measure because of the amount of time and care expended in producing them. Many segments of the population participated in the creation of cloth, beginning with the farmers who grew cotton, and those who harvested the wool of alpacas, llamas, and vicunas. In all but the most elite households, the fibers were washed, combed, dyed, and spun into yarn, then woven into panels that were sewn together—but never cut—to form everything from grain sacks and clothing to exquisite tapestries.

Most people wore simple garb—such as the man's tunic shown below left—constructed of a relatively loose woven cotton or alpaca cloth known as *huasca*. The finest fabric, called *cumbi,* was reserved for the exclusive use of the Sapa Inca, his family, and privileged individuals who had received it as a gift from the emperor. Made of soft fibers dyed in a wide range of sophisticated hues and tightly woven into standard geometric designs, cumbi garments proclaimed the wearer's status. The checkerboard and triangle yoke of the center garment, with its carefully finished seams and hem, denoted outstanding bravery or high military rank; the brilliantly colored and patterned tunic at right would have been worn by the Sapa Inca himself or his heirs.

Professional male weavers and the wives of provincial officials produced cumbi as a tax payment; special garments intended for sacred rites or to be worn by the emperor usually came from the skilled hands of women in religious service. Most weavers used the backstrap loom, which consisted of two rods—one secured with a rope *(top left)* to a fixed object such as a tree and the other attached to a belt wrapped around the waist—with the warp threads stretched between them. Cloth from such a loom thus spanned no more than an arm's length—as far as the weaver could reach in passing the weft thread through. Surviving examples of Inca textiles bespeak the intensive labor and vast quantities of material involved: An elaborate tapestry tunic could contain up to 400 threads per inch and 10 miles of yarn.

Below the Hahua Incas were the officials known as *curacas*. Successful rulers before being taken over by the Incas, they had been allowed to remain in power by their conquerors as part of the Inca practice of permitting subjugated peoples to maintain some vestige of autonomy. Under the supervision of the Inca provincial governor, they headed administrative entities composed of households.

In an attempt to achieve bureaucratic accountability, the Incas broke all the households in the empire down into neat decimal units. Every 10 households were governed by the head of one of the households. These leaders reported to heads of groups of 50 households; above them were prefects of 100, 500, 1,000, 5,000, and 10,000 households. The positions were hereditary for all those in charge of groups larger than fifty.

Thanks to this decimal hierarchy, with power reaching down through the ranks, Pachacuti could control the economies of an unwieldy assortment of communities large and small, rich and poor. Cleverly, the Incas had turned a hodgepodge of localities into relatively homogeneous economic units monitored by a chain of command that went all the way up to the Sapa Inca in Cuzco. Thus taxes could be collected and resources distributed, with relative ease. Curacas who governed a thousand or more households shared—although to a lesser extent than the noble Incas—in the bounty bestowed by the Sapa Inca upon the three top strata of society. This included gifts of land, servants, llamas, finely woven clothing, and high-status wives or concubines. The curacas also enjoyed such special privileges as the right to polygamy, to ride a litter, and to use gold and silver dishes. All were exempt from taxation. Sometimes they were even offered a wife of royal blood. In such cases, the male issue of the marriage jumped one tier in the social strata.

Making sure that taxes got paid was the primary job of the curacas. To achieve this, they took an annual count of the wealth produced in each locality, as well as a census of the people classified by age and occupation. These inventories of the work force enabled the curacas, as Garcilaso put it, "to make a judicious distribution of the tasks necessary to the public welfare."

Because there was no currency, taxes were paid in the form of fruits of labor. In territories conquered by the

Incas, all resources—farms, rivers, animal herds—were declared to be the property of the empire, and the land itself was divided into three parts. One part was to be worked by the inhabitants for their own sustenance, another for the Sapa Inca and his nobles, and the third for Inti and other Inca deities, whose beneficiaries, in fact, were the priests and other attendants of the ubiquitous Inca shrines.

Several early chroniclers, however, reported that in a province too poor to pay taxes, the Sapa Inca ordered that each household provide instead a receptacle filled with lice. Cieza de León saw this as the leader's way of getting his subjects used to paying Cuzco its due. Garcilaso's informants explained that the edict was, in fact, well intentioned; in demanding that people rid themselves of lice, the emperor was merely expressing his "love for the poor, because in this

Pumas, monkeys, llamas, lizards, and frogs, as well as human beings and gods, populate an imaginative landscape chiseled into the Saihuite Stone, a 14-foot-wide boulder on a hilltop in the Peruvian Andes. An elaborate network of miniature riverbeds and canals apparently channeled water past these figures in some sort of divination ceremony.

way these wretched people were obliged to get rid of their vermin, which in their great indigence, they might otherwise have died of."

The produce of the land was distributed to the noble Incas, and to everyone else directly employed in the service of the empire. Throughout the realm each married head of a household was guaranteed enough food for the support not just of his immediate family but of his extended one as well. "They owned nothing," said Juan Polo de Ondegardo, who served as *corregidor*, or magistrate, of Cuzco, speaking of the commoners. "Not a foot of land was theirs, but every year they were allotted land to be sown." Generous though this system was, they did have to work the plots of the emperor and Inti before attending to those earmarked for their own use. In addition, each household owed the state a levy of homespun cloth.

Unlike the farmers, specialized artisans such as jewelers, metalworkers, and potters, who lived in the towns and cities, were taxed in terms of the artifacts they produced using the raw materials the court and nobles provided them.

Found near a sun temple on an island in Lake Titicaca, this silver llama sports royal garb: a red blanket, simulated by a coloring of cinnabar, trimmed with gold. It probably represents the sacred white llama, symbol of regal authority and of the first llama on earth. The Incas regularly sacrificed llamas of various colors, especially during fertility rituals.

For the gardens of the Sapa Inca's palaces, for example, goldsmiths would place among the living plants their wondrous creations—flowers, herbs, flocks of llamas and their herders, rabbits, mice, lizards, snakes, butterflies, foxes, and wildcats, all wrought from precious metal. Garcilaso described glittering "birds set in the trees, as though they were about to sing, and others bent over the flowers, breathing in their nectar."

Still another kind of tax was demanded of the people. This was the *mit'a,* literally, a "turn," a period of time that households owed state-run enterprises. The mit'a might require a year in the army, a month spent repairing local roads, a stint in a silver or copper mine. Some localities supplied specialized mit'a; the Rucanas furnished trained litter bearers for the emperor and the Chumbivilcas sent dancers to his court. Overall, the mit'a brought the Incas an annual income of more than one billion working hours.

The custom of paying tribute through service became so deeply ingrained in the Incas that even in the later days of Spanish rule, one chronicler observed, "they resent it more when they have to give a peck of potatoes than when they work for 15 days with the community at some task."

In return for their unceasing toil, commoners enjoyed the benefits of a rudimentary welfare state, which provided for them in time of need. A large portion of the produce obtained from the land went into myriad storehouses, or *qollqas,* located in every provincial center. From these came the rations and other items that went to the widows, orphans, chronically ill, and permanently disabled on an everyday basis, and to the general population in periods of strife or catastrophe. The system sufficiently impressed Polo de Ondegardo for to him to report to his sovereign, Philip II, in the late 1500s that "it has been checked that there was relief from the Sapa Inca's warehouses" and that as a result, his subjects "never suffered hunger."

Much besides corn and potatoes was kept in the qollqas; one Spanish observer reported that Cuzco storehouses contained "shields, leather bucklers, beams for roofing houses, knives and other tools, sandals and breastplates to equip the soldiers. All was in such vast quantities that it is hard to imagine how the natives can ever have paid such immense tribute of so many items." Soldiers, recounted a chronicler, "could be entirely clothed, armed, and provided with supplies" from the depots. In return for being so well taken care of, the men were expected to show restraint; "pillaging cities was forbidden," noted Garcilaso de la Vega, "even when they had been conquered by armed force."

Partly because of the qollqas, peoples conquered by the Incas during Pachacuti's reign gained a hitherto unknown level of security. And as a result of the policies the emperor established throughout his dominions, cultures were melded, knowledge and resources were shared, and a beneficent society the likes of which had never been seen before emerged. No longer were communities plagued by internecine wars and bickering over land or water rights; no longer did the inhabitants live in mortal dread of bad harvests or natural calamities that would leave them homeless or destitute. But there was a price for so much security—a regimented, bureaucratic way of life.

Upon Pachacuti's retirement in 1471, his son, Topa Inca Yupanqui, already in command of the army, took over the rule of the empire, expanding it to almost its ultimate boundaries. By Topa Inca's death in 1493, the Inca domain would extend a length of some 2,500 miles. With Cuzco at its center, the empire included the northwestern quarter, Chinchaysuyu, with most of central and northern Peru and Ecuador inside its boundaries; the southwestern province of Cuntisuyu; Antisuyu on the heavily forested eastern slopes; and, the largest quarter of all, Collasuyu, incorporating Lake Titicaca and extending into northern Chile. At its peak, Tahuantinsuyu contained at least a hundred different ethnic groups, all of whom were pressed into the Inca mold.

What is astonishing is that Pachacuti and his successor administered this vast empire without the help of a written language. The Incas, however, developed a substitute for writing, the *quipu,* unique among human inventions and well suited to their needs. It consisted of knotted strings of cotton or wool, dyed in many colors and sometimes comprising hundreds of strands of varying lengths. Not surprisingly, its name derives from the Quechua word for knot.

Perhaps predating the Incas, the quipu became in their hands the ideal instrument of imperial control. It encoded all the statistical data the bureaucracy needed, from the total men available for mit'a work in a particular month to the quantities of corn stored in every granary in the land. Thanks to the quipu, the Incas were able to take a census of people and property so precise, according to one Spanish chronicler, that not a pair of alpaca sandals was overlooked. "The empire," wrote another chronicler, "was governed by the quipus." Andean peasants still make and use primitive quipus for noting the number of animals in their herds and the volume of their harvests.

The code the Incas used for recording numerical data on the strings was partially worked out in the early part of the 20th century by the archaeologist L. Leland Locke of New York's American Museum of Natural History. Locke's study revealed, among other things, that the Incas had a surprising understanding of important mathematical concepts, including zero. But despite Locke's brilliant work, there remains much to be learned about the quipu as a versatile and subtle medium of expression beyond being a recorder of numbers. The American ethnohistorians Marcia and Robert Ascher have painstakingly analyzed nearly half of the 400 surviving Inca quipus. Like other scholars, the Aschers believe that colors, location of the strings, and even the knots themselves may well stand for concepts, things, and verbal patterns such as the repetition of a phrase or a series of related phrases, instead of just numbers. Garcilaso noted that the quipumakers, known as *quipu camayocs*—"keepers of the quipus"— were "not only the accountants, but also the historians." He also indicated that quipus served as an aid in the memorization and recall of oral history and literature. When the dignitaries of a province wished to know some historical detail concerning their predecessors, they turned to these official rememberers who, according to Garcilaso, "never let their quipus out of their hands, and they kept passing their cords and knots through their fingers so as not to forget the tradition behind all these accounts."

The supply of ancient quipus is limited, making study of them difficult. In the late 16th century, Spanish priests burned as the devil's work every quipu they could lay their hands on. Scholars like the Aschers have had to rely on quipus recovered from graves—often by graverobbers—in coastal desert regions where the dry air has preserved the cotton or wool strings. But the fact that these come from what was only a corner of the empire rather than from its center leaves open the possibility that they may not be typical. Cuzco quipus employed at the hub of the bureaucracy probably contained far

UNRAVELING A KNOTTY CODE

To this day, researchers remain unsure of the precise information recorded on *quipus,* the knotted strings used by the Incas to tally the resources of their empire. Each individual quipu is unique, its main cord festooned with various groupings, lengths, and colors of strings *(right),* the significance of which was probably known only to the quipu's creator, who also acted as its interpreter. But in 1910, the American archaeologist L. Leland Locke deciphered a key feature shared by all quipus: The knots represent units in a base 10, or decimal, counting system, with the positions of the knots on a string indicating their place values.

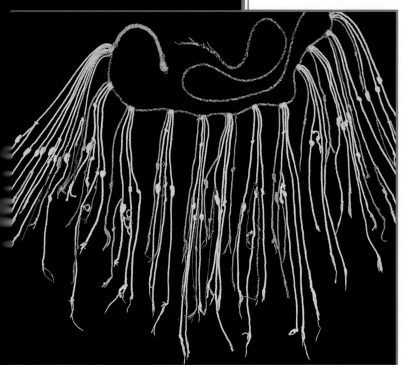

more information, but in the likelihood that any survived Spanish destruction, most by now have probably rotted away in the moister climate of the mountains.

The quipumaker is believed to have been a key cog in the bureaucracy. In shaping three-dimensional messages from string, he had to be a combination accountant, logician, and artist, and his importance presumably would have increased the closer he got to the power center in Cuzco. Indeed, the standing of quipumakers was so high, reported Garcilaso, that "they were exempted from all tribute as well as from all other kinds of service." This should not be surprising since in many cases only the person who created the quipu could read it. Despite some evidence of attempts at standardization—yellow might indicate the category *gold*, for example—the final interpretation belonged to the maker himself, who may well have intended yellow to stand for corn. The Incas considered the keeping and interpretation of the quipu such a vital calling that an error or omission was said to be punishable by death.

As controllers of numbers, the quipu camayocs were candidates for corruption, and Pachacuti recognized this. In an effort to prevent flagrant abuses of power, the Sapa Inca maintained a corps of special inspectors. Usually, they were Inca nobles responsible directly to the throne, who sometimes traveled about incognito to check up on the workings of the bureaucracy and ensure that the storehouses were full. These inquisitive inspectors bore just the right name to inspire fear in corrupt or inefficient civil servants—*tocoyricocs,* "those who see all."

Information from the tocoyricocs, as well as from the regular bureaucracy, reached the capital via the Inca system of roads. A marvel of engineering, this network, comprising more than 15,000 miles of highway, was a vital element in binding the empire together. Over it traveled the officials and agents who administered the provinces, stopping at night along the way at regularly placed stations known as *tambos,* where they would find food stored for their meals.

The roads greatly facilitated the speed of communication be-

For example, 1,705 llamas or births or ears of corn would have been recorded with one knot in the thousands position, seven knots in the hundreds position, none in the tens, and a five-looped knot in the ones position. This last was a special case that served as a reference point: The ones place never contained more than a single knot, with a figure eight to denote *one* and an extra loop for every count from two to nine.

One other feature seems clear. Subsidiary cords tied to a knotted string *(left)* probably indicated subsets of information, such as the number of men in a given group who were taxpayers.

A PICTORIAL HISTORY OF THE EMPIRE

In writing perhaps the lengthiest petition of all time—a 1,189-page letter to King Philip III describing the Inca world and protesting the iniquities of Spanish rule—Felipe Huaman Poma de Ayala helped keep a civilization from slipping into oblivion. The document, titled *Nueva Corónica y Buen Gobierno* (New chronicle and good government) was penned before 1615 in Spanish, sprinkled with transliterated Quechua.

One of a handful of accounts of Inca culture, Huaman Poma's report is especially valuable because the author illustrated his text with 400 annotated drawings *(below and right)*. Huaman Poma's visual evocations of the Incas, always busy—as indeed they were—with their daily occupations or pursuing the official business of the empire, give the viewer a more direct grasp of Andean life in this era than words alone can do.

Several of the drawings are reproduced here and throughout the book.

Born around the time of the European invasion to a mother of the Inca nobility and a father from the provincial leadership, the author witnessed firsthand the harsh methods of the conquistadors. His passionate complaint was tempered with constructive advice, however, and he recommended to Philip a government blending the best of both worlds—the Inca governmental system combined with European technology, with Christianity part of the bargain. Whether this heroic chronicle ever reached its intended recipient is unknown. After being dispatched to Spain, the manuscript vanished, only to turn up inexplicably in Copenhagen in 1908, when the German scholar Richard Pietschmann discovered it at the Royal Danish Library.

The central figure above, in the checkerboard tunic of a warrior, displays a large disk on his chest to show that he is a general. He leads men wearing Inca ear spools against enemy soldiers of Charcas.

A pair of nobles build walls symbolizing the division of land among the emperor, the religious establishment, and the community. In reality, the elite set the boundaries, and the commoners erected the walls.

The governor of royal roads, his high rank apparent in the metal trapezoid on his headband, appears to be accepting the tribute that financed his upkeep. Behind him are three tambos, or roadside shelters.

The Inca in charge of the Guambo rope bridge (foreground) allows a traveler to cross. Many workers died repairing these spans, wrote Huaman Poma, lauding the Spanish rebuilding of Inca bridges with masonry.

The son of a local leader, this swift-footed messenger blows a conch-shell trumpet and wears a conspicuous feathered headdress; both signal his approach. He is holding his weapons, a mace and a sling.

Inspecting a group of eight storehouses, or qollqas, holding cotton, coca, sweet potatoes, and corn, the emperor Topa Inca Yupanqui confers with an official who maintains a storage record on his quipu.

tween the hinterlands and the capital. Relay runners, known as *chasqui* runners, were stationed several miles apart. They constituted what Cieza de León called "a system of posts which was the best that could be thought of or imagined. It may be certain that news could not have been conveyed with greater speed on swift horses." The typical messenger, selected in his youth for speed and endurance in the thin mountain air, ran the distance to the next post at full tilt. With the white feathers on his cap streaming in the wind, he announced his approach by blowing on a conch-shell trumpet. The second runner, thus alerted, fell into stride alongside to hear and memorize the message and then carry it on to a third, who conveyed it to a fourth, and so on. News traveled at a rate of up to 250 miles a day over the network. Some messengers even conveyed fresh fish from the Pacific to the emperor's table through the relay.

But however effective all this may have been in helping to bind together his empire, Pachacuti still had to secure the loyalty of future generations if the empire as constituted was to survive his death. Shrewdly, he invited the sons of conquered provincial officials who had become curacas to attend school with the offspring of his own nobles in Cuzco. These young men eventually would go home as potential propagandists steeped in Inca pride and culture. Meanwhile, they served, like the provincial idols kept in the Coricancha, as friendly hostages to ensure the good behavior of their people.

In the hands of teachers known as *amautas,* or wise men, students learned religion, elementary geometry, history, military tactics, and oratory. With this training came indoctrination in noblesse oblige—what Garcilaso described as "the liberality and magnificence toward all that the descendants of the Sun owed to themselves as well as to their forefathers."

At age 16, the boys had to pass a series of arduous tests demonstrating their knowledge, strength, skill, and courage. These examinations lasted for a month and were conducted in the open for all to see. The participants were made to fast for six days on herbs and water and then run a four-and-a-half-mile race. Another requirement was that they stand without flinching while expert swordsmen cut and thrust within a whisker of their young faces. "They were beaten hard on the arms and legs with cane whips," Garcilaso reported, "to test their resistance to pain, and a boy who manifested the slightest

Flowers, parrots, and women in elegant dress decorate this ceramic vase—rare for its depiction of people and objects rather than abstract designs. The human figures probably represent mamaconas, *priestesses who served as ceremonial brides of the sun god, Inti, and other deities.*

sign of suffering was pitilessly banished." He also noted how, in their war games, "although they were given special weapons, less dangerous than those used in actual war, there was no lack of wounded, and, sometimes, even dead during these exercises, so ardently did these young men compete for victory."

To celebrate their successful rite of passage, graduates were honored in a ceremony at which the emperor himself presided. It was the Inca equivalent of conferring knighthood. With a golden needle, the Sapa Inca prepared them for the large ear disks of their caste. As each knelt before him, he pierced the lobes of the Inca sons and the curaca offspring. Thus the graduates took their places among the ranks of the ruling class.

Selected girls also underwent arduous training. The institution known as *acllacuna,* or chosen women, prepared females for lives as priestesses, or as attendants to the Sapa Inca himself. At any given time, there may have been as many as 15,000 chosen women in the realm. The *Acllahuasi,* or House of the Chosen Women, in Cuzco stood on the main square near the Coricancha and next to one of the Sapa Inca's most important palaces; scholars take its prime location as an indication of its significance within Inca society. Similar Acllahuasis existed at sites throughout the empire.

At about the age of ten, the chosen women were picked on the basis of beauty and skill and generally by social rank by the curacas and the Sapa Inca's agents, who scouted every locality of the empire. Those selected were taken to provincial convents and, in cloistered groups of ten, given instruction by older chosen women, the *mamaconas,* in such skills as dyeing and weaving, preparing specialty foods and *chicha* (an alcoholic drink), and conducting religious rites. Weaving had particular importance, for it was the chosen women who fashioned the exquisite cloth called *cumbi,* which they made from vicuna, alpaca, and bat wool, into garments for the emperor and his Coya.

After about three years of training, the young chosen women were subjected to a winnowing process. Each convent sent to Cuzco that year's quota of girls to attend the Festival of the Sun. There the final selection took place, with the emperor picking out those who would serve as wives, some for himself, some for his nobles. Often, these brides went to political allies and to local chieftains the ruler wanted to cultivate, "thus remunerating the services they performed for him with this sort of price," wrote the chronicler Father Cobo. A modern scholar, the ethnohistorian Irene Silverblatt of the University of Connecticut, has asserted that these women were yet another tool of Inca imperial policy—"distributed as rewards to grease the political and economic apparatus of the empire."

The remainder of the chosen women became the mamaconas, whom the Spaniards referred to as the Virgins of the Sun. They were ceremonially married to Inti and to other deities and assigned as priestesses to temples throughout the empire, where they officiated at rituals, prepared food for sacrifices, foretold the future by consulting the gods, and presided over individual shrines. They also cooked for the priests and prepared the chicha that was offered to the gods and drunk at festivals. As wives of the sun deity, mamaconas shared in the god's divinity.

Although charged along with the priests with upholding public morality, the chosen women led a far from nunlike existence. Their privileges differed little from those of priests, and as one Spanish chronicler reported, they "lived the life of great queens and ladies, and a life of tremendous pleasure and amusement, and they were very highly regarded, esteemed and loved by the Inca and by the great lords." Another Spaniard wrote that they were held in such awe and respect that no commoner "except if he were going to serve and honor them, would dare look at their faces."

The lavish Cuzco Acllahuasi—which after the conquest became a convent—housed at least 1,500 chosen women under the guidance of a high priestess who was usually one of the emperor's sisters. Harsh rules of chastity prevailed at the Houses of the Chosen Women, whether or not all who dwelled there were priestesses. Violation meant death for both partners and perhaps even destruction of the local community to which they be-

Borne on a litter by servants, the mummy of an emperor enjoys the same privileged treatment he had during life. By the time of the conquest, much of the empire's wealth went to maintaining lavish households for the royal dead.

longed. An exception was made for the emperor, who occasionally visited the House of the Chosen Women in Cuzco. If the emperor had spent the night with a mamacona, Father Cobo reported, the next morning a temple watchman would approach him in obeisance and say softly, "Last night you went into the House of the Sun, and you were with one of his women." The emperor would reply, "I sinned," and that would end the matter.

Of all the institutions introduced or strengthened by Pachacuti, perhaps the most curious was the old one of *panaca*. A panaca was the family group made up of all the descendants of an emperor in the male line, except the son who succeeded him as ruler. His successor inherited the throne but not the father's accumulated wealth, which remained the property of the dead Inca, to be managed by the panaca for the support of the relatives.

The mummy of the former Sapa Inca and his Coya symbolically headed the panaca, but its true leader was usually a brother of the new ruler. The bodies were kept propped up on thrones in the palace. Preserved through a still-unfathomed drying process that may have involved the use of herbs and wrapped in layers of fine cotton, they were dressed in sumptuous raiment and attended as if still alive. Servants looked after their every presumable need, providing offerings of food and drink and even shooing away the flies. The dead emperors—borne aloft on litters—called on one another as well as on the living Incas and their rulers, who not only worshiped them but asked their advice, with senior members of the panaca acting as go-betweens. Periodically, all the royal mummies were conveyed to the central plaza in Cuzco, and seated "in a row according to their seniority," noted Father Cobo, who wrote that with tumblers of chicha "the deceased would toast each other; the deceased would toast the living, and vice versa. The toast of the dead bodies was done in their name by the attendants."

Like his royal predecessors, Pachacuti believed that he would live forever in the form of a mummy. But the Inca practice of giving the wealth of the emperor to his descendants rather than to the prince who took over automatically obliged the new heir to add to the empire in order to amass enough lands so that he could create his own panaca. The system soon ran away with itself. Less than 50 years after Pachacuti's death, the empire was supporting almost a dozen panacas; each had hundreds of individuals connected to it, including many servants and staff members. As Pedro Pizarro, a cousin of the conquistador, wrote, "The greater part of the people and the wealth were in the possession of the dead." The expense of maintaining all those royal mummies and their relatives became too burdensome for Pachacuti's great-grandson, Huascar. But when this Sapa Inca tried to abolish the institution, he stirred up enmity among the mass of influential nobles who lived on the panaca's dole. The dissension split apart this group and put Huascar at a disadvantage in the civil war between him and his half brother, Atahualpa, that led eventually to the empire's undoing.

Immediately before the conquistadors arrived in Cuzco, the elders of the city had whisked the royal mummies out of town, and for years the Spaniards searched for them, some motivated by visions of the gold said to be hidden with them. So powerful were these relics as symbols of the vanquished Incas that the Church came to regard them as obstacles to conversion, and the colonial government viewed them as having a subversive effect.

When Cuzco's magistrate, Polo de Ondegardo, learned in 1559 that the mummies were still being worshiped in secret, he determined to find them. By interrogating an assembly of leading Inca elders, he was able to locate the bodies of three Sapa Incas, including Pachacuti's, as well as those of two Coyas, all dressed as they had been in life and seated with their arms crossed over their chests and their eyes cast down. He showed them to Garcilaso, who marveled "that not a hair, not an eyebrow, not even a lash was missing." The chronicler remembered how he touched one of the fingers of Huayna Capac, the 11th ruler, and "found it as hard as wood." He was impressed by the weight of the bodies. They were so light, he said, "that the Indians carried them in their arms with no difficulty from one house to the other to show them to the gentlemen who wanted to see them."

Polo de Ondegardo ordered the mummies sent to Lima. Garcilaso de la Vega described their dramatic departure from Cuzco: "In the street, they covered them with a white sheet; and all the Indians who saw them pass knelt down immediately and bowed, sobbing, their faces bathed in tears. Many Spaniards, too, took off their hats." The government, fearing the intense feelings the royal mummies inspired, destroyed them. Such was his greatness that even in death Pachacuti, the earthshaker, the empire builder, could pose a formidable threat to the usurpers of Inca rule.

A LASTING LEGACY IN STONE

From conquistador to modern tourist, all who have beheld the imposing ruins of the Incas have marveled at the intricacy and precision of their stonework. How a culture without benefit of written blueprints, iron tools, or the wheel could construct such sturdy monuments has long intrigued laypeople and archaeologists alike. To be sure, the Incas did not develop their skills in a vacuum; the Andean practice of building with stone predates their empire by several centuries. In fact, the Incas adopted many of their acclaimed techniques from peoples that they conquered. The area around Lake Titicaca, bristling with earlier shrines of the Tiahuanaco culture, supplied the empire with its finest masons, while the intrinsic form of an Inca living compound, the *cancha,* originated with the Huari people of the Cuzco region.

To these borrowed elements the Incas added features of their own. Doorways and decorative niches in otherwise austere walls are, as a rule, trapezoidal in shape. Joints are often beveled—for practical as well as aesthetic reasons—highlighting the individual stone blocks. The Incas also adapted their techniques to fit the wide range of climates encompassed by their empire.

Although many fine examples of Inca construction, such as the ritual chamber at Machu Picchu *(above),* involve *pirca* masonry—stones set in mud mortar—the most stunning ruins consist of massive building blocks fitted together with astonishing skill. The Incas even took their devotion to stone so far as to sculpt the natural landscape; distinctive rocks and caves were carved for ritualistic purposes with the craftsmanship that was used in temples and palaces.

Recently Jean-Pierre Protzen—an architect by profession and inquisitive by nature—set out to clarify some of the unresolved questions about Inca construction methods. Determined to take a hands-on approach, he began his quest in an abandoned Inca quarry 21 miles south of Cuzco.

ELEGANT ARTISTRY WITH THE SIMPLEST TOOLS

Scouring the ancient quarry for clues to Inca building practices, Protzen, a Swiss, discovered numerous river cobbles—egg-shaped rocks weighing from more than 20 to less than 2 pounds—with pit marks on their smaller ends, a good indication they had been used for pounding. He took up one of the heavier rocks and hammered a chunk of raw stone into a rough rectangle, then dressed the sides and squared the edges with smaller cobbles. Protzen was surprised to discover that "the process can be repeated for a long period, and the effort required is small."

From existing Inca walls, he knew that the blocks in each row have concave top faces. Protzen pounded a similar depression into the top of another large stone, then laid the convex side of his own block on top, leaving an imprint in the fine dust raised by his pounding. In some places the dust was compressed, indicating an improper fit. Through repeated pounding and fitting, he was able to match the blocks exactly.

But another mystery remains. Many of the large blocks bear protrusions, called *jetas*. Protzen suggests that these knobs may have facilitated lifting the blocks during the fitting process. But other experts point out that many jetas are sized and positioned in ways that would make them of no use as building aids. More likely, the jetas had a mystical rather than a practical function.

Stone steps and a massive retaining wall at the Sacsahuaman bastion exemplify the Incas' penchant for lofty design. The rounded cornerstones have a graceful, almost pillowy look despite their immense size, while the beveled joints cast deep shadows in the bright Andean sunshine.

A classic example of polygonal construction—randomly shaped blocks fitted together like pieces in a jigsaw puzzle—this wall in Cuzco includes one stone with 12 angled sides. The block nestles so tightly against its neighbors that a knife cannot penetrate the joints between them.

This elegant doorway lies below the Temple of the Sun at Ollantaytambo. The surrounding wall embodies the culmination of the polygonal style. Its blocks bear many of the enigmatic jetas, whose purpose remains shrouded in doubt.

Set in a wall of coursed masonry—smooth, symmetrical blocks in perfectly straight rows—this trapezoidal wall niche in Cuzco's Coricancha (golden enclosure) represents some of the finest Inca stonework. Tiny holes in the niche's frame were used for affixing gold plates, which adorned the temple in great quantities.

HARMONY OF STRUCTURE AND ENVIRONMENT

While few traces remain of the crude mud dwellings that housed the vast majority of the population, there exist ruins of upper-class domiciles and imperial administrative centers that demonstrate how Inca architecture reflected the diverse environments of the Andean region.

Along the empire's arid coast, scarce rainfall allowed adobe to predominate and roofs to be laid flat. The only feature that distinguishes Inca buildings here from earlier or later construction is the ubiquitous use of trapezoid-shaped doors and niches.

In this temperate zone, the conventional pattern of the cancha—the residential compound—evolved. The cancha consisted of living quarters and storage buildings grouped around a central courtyard. When this layout was transferred to the wetter, colder, windy highlands, the courtyard was retained, but the roofs acquired gables for deflecting rain, and stone supplanted adobe.

Examples of state-sponsored construction of the time done under bureaucratic auspices also reflect climatic considerations and a certain uniformity of style.

These desolate walls mark the site of a cancha not far from Machu Picchu belonging to a member of the Inca elite. The buildings are of the stone-and-mud-mortar construction called pirca, *the most common form of Inca masonry. The stone gables once supported steeply pitched, thatched roofs to facilitate rainwater runoff in this wet climate.*

Perched on a hillside at Ollantaytambo, this complex of buildings is thought to have been either a storehouse for the area's inhabitants or barracks for an Inca garrison. Staggered one above the other, each building commands breathtaking views of the Urubamba valley from numerous large windows. Individually, the buildings impart a light and airy aspect. As a whole, the cluster merges naturally into the slope and seems altogether appropriate for its mountain setting.

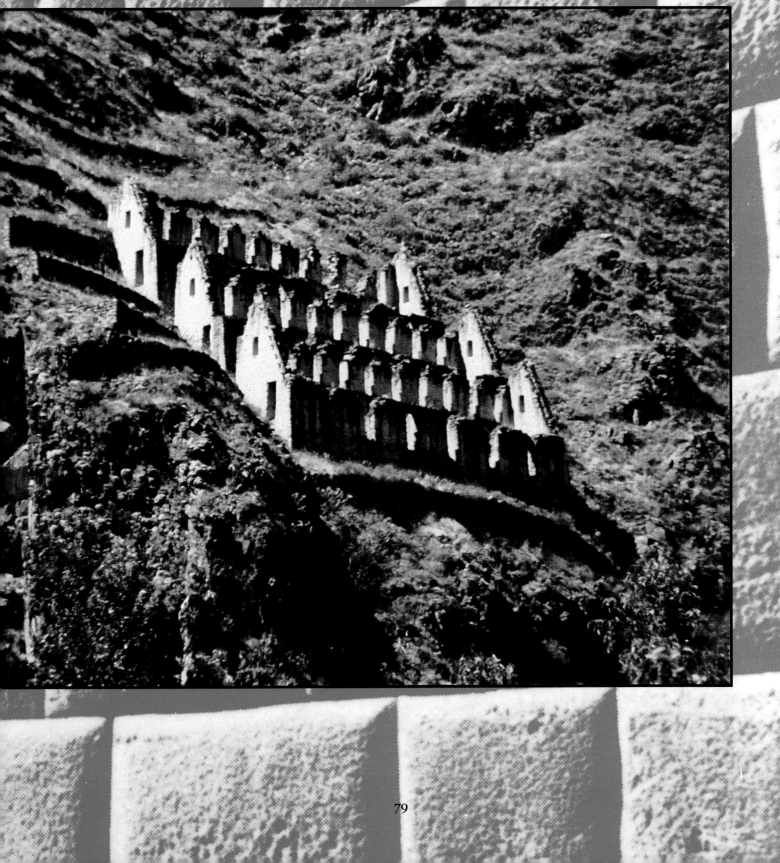

Flanked by sturdy walls, the royal retreat at Pisac—only a small segment of which is shown here—exhibits coursed masonry of red volcanic stone. The semicircular wall (center) is the ruin of the palace's Temple of the Sun. Terraces surrounding the central buildings were put under cultivation, mostly for growing corn, and also served to hinder an enemy's approach. Commissioned by Pachacuti, Pisac's design suggests it functioned as a fortress as well as an imperial residence.

MAJESTIC PALACES FOR THE MOVABLE COURT

During the heyday of the Inca empire, its supreme rulers built several opulent estates in the countryside around Cuzco. Accompanied by his retinue of courtiers, an emperor could retire to one of his pastoral retreats and conduct state business away from the hustle and bustle of the capital.

The great ruler Pachacuti was responsible for some of the finest of these country residences. He chose locales that appealed to him for their scenic beauty and then, by royal fiat, mobilized the empire's unlimited labor force to realize the projects. Pachacuti's private estates remained in the hands of his descendants for generations after his death.

But these sites were more than just a home away from home for the godlike Inca leader; the surrounding acreage was terraced and put under cultivation with miles of irrigation canals to augment his worldly wealth.

Such was the efficiency of Inca agricultural methods that food production from these lands not only supplied the needs of the permanent staff and the visiting bureaucracy but also generated a surplus, which, under the strict tenets of Inca hierarchy, became the personal property of the ruler himself.

Pachacuti's lodge stood on the site of this spring at Tambo Machay. Channels carved into the polygonal retaining walls created fountains for the sacred waters. The niches in the upper wall possibly once held religious idols, testifying to the spring's spiritual significance.

Hugging the sheer face of a cliff, the dizzying road to Machu Picchu typifies the Incas' mastery of engineering techniques. The trail was deliberately laid along this vertiginous route for defensive reasons; where logs now span the chasm at center, a drawbridge once served as a strategically placed checkpoint.

REVERENCE FOR THE LIVING ROCK

The Incas regarded stone not only as a strong and abundant building material, but also with undisguised spiritual devotion. In the barren highlands that spawned Inca theology, stone is omnipresent. The stark pinnacles of the surrounding Andes formed the axis of the Incas' known universe, and rocky outcrops punctuated the landscape throughout their realm. Many of these geological features were deemed *huacas*—mystical places that possessed inherent powers of their own.

It is no wonder, then, that the unsurpassed skills of the Inca stonemasons were applied to natural rock formations—for both utilitarian and religious purposes.

Using the same type of stone tools and techniques with which Protzen experimented on freestanding building blocks, these long-vanished, anonymous craftsmen created monuments to their culture that have survived Spanish depredation, massive earthquakes, and half a millennium of wind and rain.

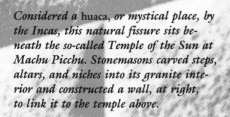

Considered a huaca, *or mystical place, by the Incas, this natural fissure sits beneath the so-called Temple of the Sun at Machu Picchu. Stonemasons carved steps, altars, and niches into its granite interior and constructed a wall, at right, to link it to the temple above.*

Broad ledges cut into a rocky hilltop overlooking the fortresslike temple of Sacsahuaman were once referred to as the Throne of the Inca. Current scientific opinion, however, holds that the site had a spiritual function and was probably used for either the placement of sacrifices or the performance of religious rituals.

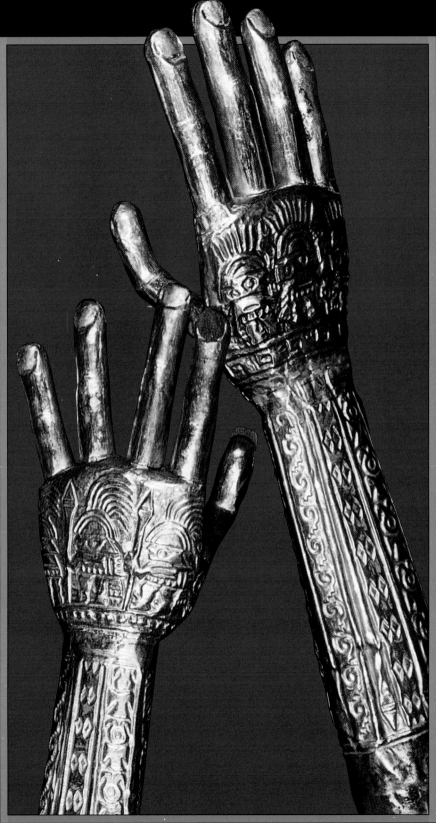

BORROWERS OF GREATNESS

These hammered-gold gauntlets probably sheathed the hands of a noble Chimu mummy. The designs—warriors in battle dress and geometric patterns—reflect the Chimu practice of tattooing their bodies.

Mighty empire builders though they may have been, the Incas were not quite all that they seemed to the conquering Spaniards, who confessed such amazement over their achievements. What the Spaniards did not know is that the Incas had been quick to appropriate the technology of others. Virtually all the marvels of their civilization—from the great stone structures at Cuzco, to the agricultural terraces of the mountain slopes, to the 15,000 miles of paved highways that knitted the empire together— took their inspiration from earlier ethnic groups. Even the magnificent gold artifacts that so enchanted the Spaniards were largely the work of other hands.

Not that the Incas gave much credit. As their court historians told it, little of consequence had occurred in the Andes before the Incas' rise to power. Whatever culture the region enjoyed, they implied, had originated with the Incas. The truth is that civilized life in the Andes went back at least 3,000 years. Archaeologists have found temples in the highlands and great cities in the coastal deserts that were as remote in time from the age of Inca greatness as is the Athens of Pericles from the Athens of modern Greece. But if the Incas were inheritors, they were able to mark the accomplishments of those who preceded them with the stamp of their own genius.

From the beginning, life in the areas that would become the

Inca empire posed unique challenges to the Indians who inhabited them. In valleys leading to the coastal desert, for example, the climate was so dry that no more than an inch or two of rain fell in any single year. While some groups made their living along the coast as fishermen, harvesting the rich protein bounty churned up by the colder temperatures of the currents sweeping north from Antarctica, others in the valleys tended garden plots of squash and beans, and eventually corn, on small green patches made possible by water from rivers gushing from the heights. Settlement spread as people began moving inland, there to meet other challenges posed by the extremes of weather and altitude. Towns grew up around ceremonial centers, then turned into cities filled with all the creative bustle of civilized Stone Age life. As long ago as 2500 BC (and perhaps before), early Peruvians, working in adobe brick, built temple pyramids in various coastal areas of Peru that rival Egypt's in their monumental scale. A spectacular example of these, carbon-dated to 1800-1500 BC, stands 10 stories tall at a site called Pampa de las Llamas-Moxeke.

One of the first students of Andean culture to explore this ancient progression was the German archaeologist Max Uhle. As early as the 1890s, Uhle commenced digging at various burial sites in the mountains and along the Pacific coast, unearthing pottery and textiles and comparing their decorative motifs. His findings enabled him to sketch out a relative chronology of ancient Peruvian styles.

A site that fascinated Uhle was Tiahuanaco, known for its ancient and mysterious set of megalithic monuments near the shores of Lake Titicaca in present-day Bolivia. Titicaca, at 12,500 feet above the Pacific, is the world's highest body of navigable water, and one of the most remote. The surrounding puna, or treeless tableland, is bleak beyond imagining—a plateau of rock and hardy ichu grass, swept by bitter high-country winds, and stretching to a fringe of distant mountain ranges. The region is said to have four seasons per day: Spring when the sun rises, summer at noon, autumn in the evening, and winter as the frigid mountain darkness settles in.

But the ruins that stand near Lake Titicaca are astonishing. Uhle made drawings and ground plans of what were probably three limestone temples and four administrative structures, set on a series of raised platforms and in sunken rectangular courts. Like all visitors who come here, he marveled at the edifices' monolithic stonework.

First detected in 1931, this rampart cuts across the Andean foothills through the southern portion of the Kingdom of Chimor. What had looked like disjointed piles of rock and adobe from the ground emerged as a linear barrier 50 miles long when finally viewed from the air.

Some of the blocks are as big as small rooms and weigh up to 100 tons. They were cut and fitted with such precision that mortar was not used, nor even necessary. Already in ruins by the time the Incas took over the region in the 15th century, a legend arose that Tiahuanaco had been erected at the dawn of time, by a race of gods or giants.

Little is known about the Tiahuanacans and their culture. But archaeology, using carbon dating, has provided a specific time frame for their monuments. The Tiahuanaco temple complex began taking shape, it seems, around the first century AD, then expanded 500 years later and continued to grow for another five centuries. Among the legacies of this mysterious culture is a massive doorway, the Gate of the Sun, hewn from a single block of stone. Carved on its lintel is the figure of a god with round, staring eyes, and a halo of serpent and feline heads. In each hand is a staff, one tipped with a condor head. The god's image appears not only at Tiahuanaco, but throughout the Peruvian Andes. Uhle, excavating at Pachacamac, a shrine on the coast near Lima that had been revered from ancient times through the Inca period, found an abundance of Tiahuanacan motifs. In coastal ruins to the north, close to the city of Trujillo, he uncovered further images of the deity. Clearly, Tiahuanaco had spread its influence across much of the territory later occupied by the Incas.

To the north of Tiahuanaco lay the empire of the Huari, so named after the ruins of their capital city. This highland polity dominated the very region where the Incas would come to power. The Huari flourished during the same period as the Tiahuanacans, and they too had disappeared as a political force by Inca times. Their physical legacy consisted of the fieldstone walls of their well-planned cities and bureaucratic posts and the network of interconnecting roadways between them.

Before its disappearance, the Huari empire stretched north from the valley of Cuzco nearly to the border of present-day Ecuador, and from the central cordillera down to the coast. Its influence is recognizable in the urban planning of the Chimu, a dynasty arising around the ninth century AD. When Topa Inca Yupanqui, the 10th ruler of the Incas, conquered the Kingdom of Chimor between 1465 and 1470, he took over a culture that in some respects was considerably more advanced than his own. The adobe-brick capital of Chan Chan was one of the largest cities in South America, with a population of perhaps 36,000 people. Chimu croplands, in the river valleys bordering the coastal deserts, were watered by an irrigation system of unequaled scope and efficiency. Chimu craftsmen were among the best in America; much of the Inca gold that later bedazzled the conquistadors was wrought by Chimu hands. Confronted by such displays of wealth and talent, the Incas did the wise thing—they absorbed the Chimu culture, getting their artisans to work for them and thus becoming, in a way, the disciples of their own vassals.

When the great Pachacuti came to power, he had the opportunity to see firsthand achievements of the other Andean cultures, past and present, as he marched from conquest to conquest. Like the Spaniards, he could only have been impressed, and it is possible that he found himself wishing not only to duplicate some of their accomplishments but also to surpass their collective imperial grandeur. Early on he launched the rebuilding of Cuzco. The city apparently had developed as a haphazard cluster of modest fieldstone dwellings, many of them one-room structures. Pachacuti swept these away, then laid out a roughly rectangular street plan, replacing the earlier structures with palaces and temples, including the bastionlike Sacsahuaman temple. For his model, he looked to the civic monuments of two earlier cultures: the temples at Tiahuanaco, and the great walled compounds of the Huari.

The lords of Huari were in some respects the Incas' closest cultural ancestors. Both were highlanders, both conquerors; and like the Incas, they seem to have kept their subjects on a fairly tight rein, sending out orders and accepting tribute along miles of well-tended roadways. Above all, the Huari were consummate builders—the first true urban planners in South America. They laid out one of their administrative centers, Pikillacta, only 17 miles southeast of Cuzco, with the foursquare precision of a military encampment, with more than 700 buildings of monumental stature, many as large as three stories high and 150 feet long. The walls of these structures consisted of fieldstone set in mud cement smoothed over with coats of clay and gypsum plaster; from

Modern Peruvian archaeology began with the German Max Uhle (right), the first scholar to document a long succession of Andean cultures that predated the Incas. One of the sites he investigated was Tiahuanaco (below), the ceremonial center of a civilization that flourished in the first millennium AD. Through Uhle's efforts, much information about the achievements of this prodigious and enigmatic people, long the subject of fanciful legends, has come to light.

the evidence of surviving ruins, some measured 6 feet thick and rose up nearly 50 feet from their foundations. A system of underground conduits provided drainage for the complex.

Several archaeologists believe that Pachacuti took his general city plan from Pikillacta. He seems to have lifted directly both the street grid and the basic layout of the *cancha,* an enclosed dwelling area with an interior courtyard that became standard for dwellings in the Inca imperial style. But Cuzco's true glory lay not in its mimicry of Huari order but in the perfectly crafted cut-stone blocks that formed its finest buildings. And for these the inspiration was drawn from the monuments of Tiahuanaco.

Like its Tiahuanaco counterpart, Inca stonework is massive and finely hewn. The Incas cut some blocks jigsaw fashion; one famous stone in the wall of the Hatun Rumiyoc, the palace of the sixth ruler, Inca Roca, displays no fewer than 12 corners on its outer face, all interlocking perfectly with the adjoining stones. For other walls, they finished stones of uniform size and laid them in even rows like brickwork. To ensure that such stones would fit and hold, they made the top of each slightly concave, forming a saucerlike depression that would cradle the stone above, which bulged out on its bottom surface. By keying or locking stones together at the point of greatest strain they created walls that could withstand earthquakes; the tremors might lift the stones briefly, but the stones would just as quickly settle down into position. Even more astonishing is how the Incas managed to cut the gigantic blocks seen in their surviving structures in Cuzco and elsewhere. "They are as big as forest tree trunks," wrote Pizarro's secretary, Pedro Sancho, of the huge foundation stones of the Sacsahuaman fortified temple. "Three carts could not carry even the smallest of them." He did not exaggerate—one of the stones is estimated to weigh 86 tons, another 126 tons, and one is so large that if it were hollow, three carts could fit inside it. Another chronicler,

El Inca Garcilaso de la Vega, who had spent his boyhood scrambling about Sacsahuaman's ramparts, thought a casual observer might "even believe that they were made by some form of magic—built by demons rather than men."

Men did build them, of course, and the chroniclers tell not only who, but how. According to Cieza de León, 20,000 conscripts worked each year on constructing and reinforcing Cuzco's fortifications as part of their annual labor tax. "Four thousand of them quarried and cut the stones," he wrote. "Six thousand hauled these with great cables of leather and hemp; others dug the ditch and laid the foundations; while still others cut poles and beams for the roof timbers." Overseeing these laborers were the master architects and stonemasons, working from clay models. Most of the stoneworkers were recruited from the region of Tiahuanaco and came with skills that had been passed down to them from their ancestors.

The sheer physical effort expended at every stage of construction must have been extraordinary. Just getting the stone to the site called for enormous energy and ingenuity. Cuzco's architects favored

Tiahuanaco's massive Gate of the Sun was cut from a single block of stone weighing perhaps 100 tons. An even greater challenge for the builders than carving the portal was bringing this and the other monoliths of Tiahuanaco to the site from a quarry miles away. Archaeologists speculate that the blocks may have been pulled to their location along roadbeds of logs or smooth, round pebbles.

90

three types of stone, only one of them native to the immediate area. A greenish diorite like that used in Sacsahuaman's outer walls, for example, could be taken from nearby outcrops; but the limestone blocks of the citadel's foundations had to be dragged nine miles overland. And for most temples and palaces the architects ordered up andesite, a granitelike rock, that probably was brought from Rumiqolqa, 21 miles to the southeast.

The Spaniards were deeply impressed by the building skills of the Incas. Father Bernabé Cobo, writing of his fellow countrymen's reaction to their architecture, said: "What amazes us the most when we look at these buildings is to wonder with what tools and apparatus could they take these stones out of the rocks in the quarries, work them, and put them where they are without implements made of iron, nor machines with wheels, nor using either the ruler, the square, or the plumb bob, nor any of the other kinds of equipment and implements that our artisans use."

At the quarries, workers pried the stones loose from bedrock, either jamming bronze crowbars into natural fault lines or driving in wooden wedges that were then soaked with water to make them swell and cause a crack to form. Cutters trimmed the resulting blocks to the general size needed, readying them for transport to Cuzco. Not all the stones made it there. Numbers of semi-finished blocks still litter several of the ancient routes—some famous ones near Ollantaytambo have long been referred to as the Piedras Cansadas—"tired stones."

Once they had been dragged to the construction site, the blocks were hauled into position up dirt ramps. It has been conservatively estimated that it would take at least 2,400 men to move the heaviest of the stones to the top of a ramp, a figure that corroborates Cieza de León's account of the number of workers at Sacsahuaman. But even before being muscled into place, each block had to be shaped to an exact fit.

How did they do it? Other than their crowbars, the Inca stoneworkers had no iron or steel tools—no mallets, no grinding wheels. About all they had were cobblestones, harder than the blocks themselves, and they used these like hammers to pound the rock into shape. But all the grueling hours of backbreaking labor paid off. Inca construction is as stable as the bedrock from which the stones came—"so strong,"

Carved with meticulous detail, Tiahuanacan deities decorated the huge doorways of the city. Many of the figures display tear tracks below their eyes—a feline characteristic—perhaps evoking the puma, which was sacred to many Andean cultures. That corresponding images have been found on pottery and textiles all over the Andes as far away as the north coast of Peru is evidence to some archaeologists that Tiahuanaco's cultural influence was widespread.

BRAIN SURGERY BEFORE ITS TIME IN ANCIENT PERU

When Ephraim George Squier, an American diplomat and anthropologist, traveled to Peru in 1863, he had little notion that he was embarking on a voyage of discovery. He was merely looking for antiquities.

But then, on a visit to a private archaeological collection, Squier saw an Inca skull with a large rectangular piece missing. Squier's curiosity was piqued, and he bought the relic. Eventually he sent it to the famed French anatomist and physical anthropologist Paul Broca. When Broca received Squier's acquisition, he immediately recognized its uniqueness. Never before had the scientist seen such precision in removing bone from an ancient skull.

Trephination, the cutting out of portions of the cranium, was practiced in Africa as long as 12,000 years ago, and in Europe at least 6,000 years ago. However, those excisions had been mostly from the skulls of dead people and were performed probably for superstitious reasons, such as the letting out of evil spirits. Broca concluded that the operation on the Inca skull had been carried out on living bone tissue, as was evidenced by signs of infection around the edges of the opening. It seemed obvious that the operation had been done for some sort of medical reason. Later studies of other trephined Peruvian skulls have disclosed a variety of daring surgical techniques and have revealed the startling fact that more than half of the patients who underwent trephination completely healed.

Scientists have determined that the hundreds of trephined skulls found in Peru to date outnumber all of the known prehistoric trephined skulls in the rest of the world. Something unusual had been going on in Peru centuries before the advent of modern medicine—and it was brain surgery.

Rectangular incisions such as this one were made by cutting grooves deeper and deeper into the skull until the loosened piece could be lifted out.

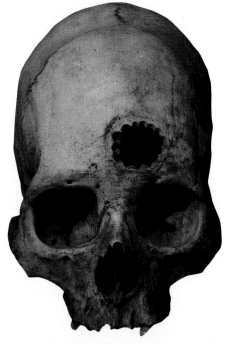

Drilling, cutting, and scraping through bone to get at the brain, Peruvian surgeons used tools such as knives, tweezers, chisels, hammers, and scalpels (left) with remarkably great precision.

Examples of trephinations made by drilling and cutting, as in the example shown here, are rare; not surprisingly, the patient usually died before the surgeon could complete the incision.

Circular cutting was the most successful trephination technique. Two views of one skull (above) reveal that the surgeon kept enlarging circular grooves until a wafer of bone could be removed. This patient, who endured five such procedures, with each trephination showing evidence of healing, probably suffered from recurrent headaches. The first Peruvian trephinations were done around 400 BC; techniques improved as surgeons learned from their predecessors' fatal errors.

Despite extensive damage to this skull, the victim, on whom a trephination was done, lived, as is indicated by the healing of the bone. The purpose of many such operations carried out in Peru was to treat not only head injuries but also neurological problems, such as epilepsy.

wrote another admiring Spaniard, "that it will last for as long as the world exists." And so far it has, in this land of earthquakes and avalanches, except where the Spaniards raided the old sites for construction materials.

Although the strengths of Inca architecture have been characterized as "simplicity, symmetry, and solidity," there is beauty and elegance inherent in the design. Among the many outstanding examples are the aesthetically pleasing walls of coursed masonry blocks of Cuzco's Acllahuasi, the House of the Chosen Women, that gradually decrease in size toward the top, or the apselike, bowed retaining wall of the city's Coricancha, the "golden enclosure." And El Torreón, a dramatic semicircular landmark at Machu Picchu, exemplifies the melding of art with ingenuity. The wall that connects the curving tower with a two-and-a-half-story house is composed of granite blocks that, while they may look rectangular, do not have a right angle or straight line among them. By alternating the nearly rectangular stones with keyed or locked ones, the Inca master masons created a series of braces that have kept the wall flush to its adjoining structures to this day.

Not all Inca buildings were royal monuments like these, though, and large numbers of purely functional, yet imposing, structures dotted the countryside. Take, for example, the *qollqas,* the storehouses for grain, clothing, tools, and weapons placed strategically along the highways and outside the provincial capitals. Most were built of mud-plastered fieldstone, often in the silolike shape of some traditional village dwellings. They stood in great formal clusters on the hillsides, where rain drained off quickly, their contents dry and ready for use in case of famine or civic unrest.

Almost as remarkable as the stone cities, royal retreats, and storehouses and other administrative buildings of the Incas was the network of highways that linked them. An Inca ruler could travel the length of his dominion, from Ecuador to Chile, and except for the crossing of a few major rivers his litter bearers would never need to step from the well-tended roadbed.

The stone-paved roads of Tahuantinsuyu are often compared to those of the Roman Empire. Both were used to maintain control of diverse groups living far from the capital. But even the Romans did not have to travel routinely through tangled masses of tropical jungle, over mountains more than 20,000 feet high, and across raging torrents of rivers hundreds of feet wide.

In the aerial photograph below, the Huari provincial capital of Pikillacta reveals the fastidious standardized pattern common to all imperial Huari settlements. But rigidity was abandoned when the Huari turned to art. A mosaic of shell and stone adorns the back of a mirror (left), and a carved wooden scepter (right) includes a shell-inlay likeness of a nobleman surrounded by war clubs.

Two main arteries, linked by numerous connecting roads, coursed through the empire, one along the coast and the other through the highlands. The coast road started in Ecuador's palm-fringed Gulf of Guayaquil and swung down through the desert littoral, near the Chimu capital of Chan Chan, on past the shrines of Pachacamac, through the dry sands of Nazca, ending 3,000 miles later at Chile's Maule River, just south of present-day Santiago. The highland route, called the Capac-nan, or royal road, stretched even farther, from the mountains north of Quito, down through the battlefields of the great Inca conquests, past the plaza of Cajamarca, scene of Atahualpa's capture, then along the Mantaro River, where Huascar was captured and murdered, across the Apurimac River and into Cuzco. From there the road continued south, arrowing across the altiplano, skirting Lake Titicaca, climbing up through the high passes of Bolivia, and reaching its terminus near Tucumán, in Argentina. The two systems, counting the mountain roads that linked them, and the offshoots reaching through the montaña into the lowland jungles, stretched more than 15,000 miles.

Portions of these highways had been laid down centuries earlier by the Huari and, in the north, by the Chimu and others. But the Incas expanded and improved them. Causeways built of adobe or of blocks of stone raised roadbeds over marshy ground, with stone-laid cul-

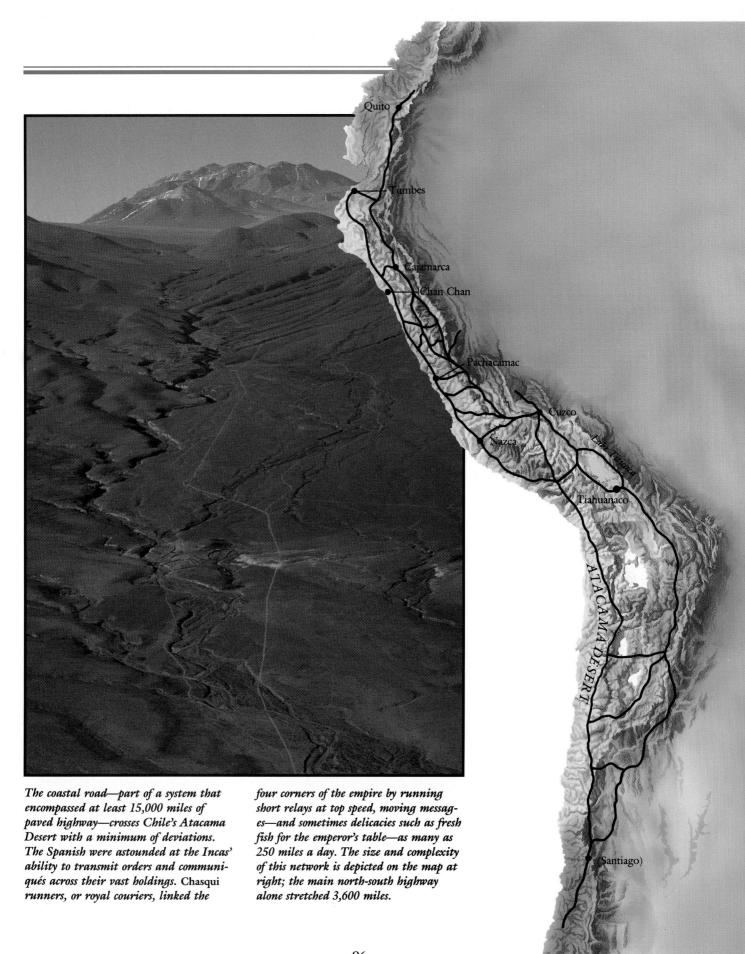

The coastal road—part of a system that encompassed at least 15,000 miles of paved highway—crosses Chile's Atacama Desert with a minimum of deviations. The Spanish were astounded at the Incas' ability to transmit orders and communiqués across their vast holdings. Chasqui runners, or royal couriers, linked the four corners of the empire by running short relays at top speed, moving messages—and sometimes delicacies such as fresh fish for the emperor's table—as many as 250 miles a day. The size and complexity of this network is depicted on the map at right; the main north-south highway alone stretched 3,600 miles.

Quito

Tumbes

Cajamarca

Chan Chan

Pachacamac

Cuzco

Nazca

Lake Titicaca

Tiahuanaco

ATACAMA DESERT

(Santiago)

verts ensuring proper drainage. Elsewhere, surfaces might be plastered with a tough, weatherproof compound of corn leaves, pebbles, and clay. Along the hardpan of the coast the road was left unpaved; but stone pillars marked the shoulders, and along some stretches low walls of stone or adobe were built to keep out the sand and to prevent the llama caravans or relay messengers from straying. On the main routes, boundary stones marked the distances.

Road widths varied with the terrain, from nearly 20 feet in the flats, along the desert and puna, down to 3 feet in the mountain passes. Wherever possible, the roads were laid out with linear precision. The Inca engineers seemed to prefer to surmount obstacles rather than evade them. And since the highways were used only by pedestrians or surefooted llamas, there was virtually no limit on the steepness of the gradient. This made for rugged travel in the highlands, involving switchbacks, dizzying flights of stairs, and even ladders cut into bedrock. On the route between Machu Picchu and Vilcabamba, where the path hugs the side of a mountain escarpment, a 12-foot-high man-made stone embankment carries the roadway. At another place, the road passes through a tunnel-like rock cut, 15 feet long, made by enlarging a natural fissure. The sloping tunnel is tall enough for a man to walk through and has low steps cut into its floor.

The road builders faced their toughest challenge, however, when spanning the region's numerous waterways. Although many rivers were fordable, some were so swift that crossing was difficult even where the water was only knee-deep. Narrow rivers or small streams on level ground could be bridged with logs or with corbeled stone archways. Wide, slow-moving rivers called for a different approach—pontoon bridges made from highly buoyant reed boats, tethered together and covered by a wooden roadbed. When it came to spanning the deep river gorges of the montaña, the road builders often rigged an *oroya*, a kind of cable car that hung from a heavy rope of twisted vines or ichu grass strung from one bank to the other. The passenger, crouching in a reed basket that dangled from the cable, would be pulled across by men on the far side. But sometimes there was no basket, and Father Cobo tells what happened then: "They just tie the man securely so that if he becomes alarmed and faints, he cannot fall, and hanging in the air from the cable by a large wooden hook, he is pulled from one side to the other."

Taking the most direct route up and over the region's innumerable mountains, Inca roadways included dizzying stairways and cliff-face paths cut into living rock. Chasqui *runners and hardy llamas were undaunted by the heart-stopping gradients, but Spanish conquistadors found them a formidable barrier to the safe and swift passage of their cavalry.*

While this makeshift basket arrangement worked fine for individual travelers on secondary roads, major highways demanded something more substantial. To carry people and cargo across the mountain torrents, the Incas built suspension bridges. These rank among the outstanding triumphs of their engineering. A pair of stone pylons was raised on either bank to anchor a set of massive cables woven of ichu grass, each "thick as the body of a boy," according to Cobo. Two cables functioned as guardrails; three others supported the roadbed, made of plaited branches. The bridges sagged from their own weight, and they swayed alarmingly in the wind. But they were strong enough to support nobles carried in their litters and, later, the Spaniards with their horses. To ensure safety, the cables were replaced at least once a year by local villagers whose only task was to keep them in repair. The most spectacular of the bridges, slung over the Apurimac canyon on the main road north from Cuzco, reached 220 feet from bank to bank, while the river churned 118 feet below.

For all the high drama attendant upon using the Inca highways, their builders strove to make travel swift and pleasant. Along some stretches they planted fruit trees watered by means of irrigation ditches; travelers could pick the fruit for refreshment. The builders erected tambos (roadside shelters) at intervals of 15 to 30 miles, and provided corrals for llamas. At each, a local caretaker kept stocks of provisions—corn, lima beans, dried potatoes, dried meat. Recent archaeological investigations reveal that the Incas constructed and maintained tambos on every road throughout the empire, totaling around 1,000 in all. Colonial records report an attempt by the Spaniards to keep the tambos going as an integral part of the highway network, but with far less success than the Incas had had.

These way stations, like the qollqas, illustrate the importance of storage to the smooth running of the Inca empire. But they would have been of little use had the Incas not created an effective agricultural economy. To take care of the food needs of the burgeoning empire, they had to reshape entire landscapes—and they did so by terracing mountainsides, straightening rivers, filling or draining marshes, and channeling water into the deserts to make them bloom. In a realm that was mostly vertical and whose horizontal stretches tended to be either arid steppe or outright desert, few areas lent themselves readily to farming.

Agricultural terraces can be seen throughout the empire—

Made of 22,000 feet of hand-braided ichu grass, this authentic modern reconstruction of an Inca suspension bridge is anchored to the original stone abutments on either side of the gorge. These graceful spans represented the pinnacle of Inca highway engineering. Local peasants performed continual maintenance on the structures as part of their mit'a, *or obligation to public service.*

climbing up the mountainsides that surround Cuzco, along broad stretches of the Colca valley to the south, and at hundreds of other steeply angled locations in the Inca realm. Some 2.5 million acres were carved out this way, making farming possible where it could not have been conducted before. (In Peru today only about 6 million acres of land are regularly cultivated.) According to legend, credit for the building of the terraces goes to Pachacuti, though some of the work predates the Inca dynasty. The Incas, however, raised the construction of these *andenes,* as they are called, almost to an art form.

Typical andenes are 5 to 13 feet high, width and length varying according to the steepness of the terrain. Some measure 50 to 200 feet wide and as much as 5,000 feet long at the bottom of the incline, but since they narrow as they rise, they may be only big enough on top for a few rows of corn or vegetables. Most terrace walls are of fieldstone, and as reported by Garcilaso, "they slope back slightly so as to withstand the weight of earth with which they are filled." Others—near Cuzco, for example—were fashioned from the same type of cut-stone blocks that were used to construct the royal palaces.

After building the retaining walls, laborers poured in rubble fill to ensure proper drainage, then dumped on top thousands of loads of earth carried up from the valleys in baskets strapped to their backs. The fertility of the soil was ensured in some places by the use of guano (bird droppings), which was imported from roosting areas on islands off the coast when unavailable locally. To link terraces— some of which rose as high as one-story houses—farmers constructed steps. In some places they inserted stone slabs in the walls, whose projecting ends could serve as ladders. Since irrigation was absolutely essential to growing crops, channels bringing water from rivers fed from glacial heights were created, with conduits dug or cut in and along the terraces to allow the liquid to flow freely from one level to another. Archaeologists theorize that the abandonment of many of the ancient andenes was due to depopulation of the area.

Throughout much of the Inca empire usable water was a scarce commodity. And nowhere was this problem more acute than in the arid agricultural lands along the coast. The earliest farmers sought relief by digging down into the sand. Eventually reaching the level of the water table, they would plant beans and squash where moisture percolated up. But a growing population required more

The curious terraces of Moray, huge cone-shaped depressions cut 33 feet into the limestone plateau northwest of Cuzco, are a singular example of Inca agronomy. Speculation abounds as to their purpose. They could have served as open-air hothouses for growing coca, which thrives in direct sunshine, sheltered from the wind. Alternatively, the site could have been an agricultural research station since each terrace, from top to bottom, encompasses 20 distinct climatic zones.

ambitious measures. Forced by need, the inhabitants developed the most extensive and enduring irrigation system in pre-Columbian America. In the area of the Moche River, early Peruvians dug a number of deep trenches through the sands of the upper valley, with offshoots leading to cornfields on the slopes below. Not only did the trenches channel water from the cordillera during its rainy season, from November through May, but they also helped to raise the water table in the lowlands as the liquid gradually soaked down through the sands and accumulated there. Besides corn, local farmers could now raise beans, squash, peppers, fruit trees, and cotton.

When the Chimu came to power in the northern coastal area during the ninth century, they chose for their capital Chan Chan, a desert littoral where major rainfalls occur only every 40 or 50 years. The need to provide food for Chan Chan's many inhabitants made the Kingdom of Chimor a totally hydraulic society, that is, one

WATER—THE LIFEBLOOD OF CIVILIZATION

Inca legend held that Mama Micay, the wife of Inca Roca, saw that the valley surrounding Cuzco lacked sufficient water to irrigate the cornfields, so she magically brought water to the city. Apocryphal though the story may be, Spanish chroniclers noted that Mama Micay's "family and lineage" controlled the vital water rights to the Cuzco area.

Although the Incas took credit in their mythology for the first use of irrigation, massive diversion and conservation projects had in fact been carried out by earlier cultures, especially the Chimu. All types of waterworks, however, reached their zenith under the skillful and efficient hand of the Incas.

Only a dry serpentine bed remains of a great canal that once linked the Moche and Chicama river valleys. The parched region receives less than an inch of rain a year, but the Chimu were able to tap the abundant flow of Andean rivers and make the desert grow corn.

Seldom content with the hand that nature dealt them, the Incas reworked the landscape to suit their own purposes. A striking example is the Urubamba River, whose meandering path their engineers straightened. They also graded the valley floor to produce many more acres of flat, cultivable land.

Viracocha, the Creator in Inca theology, was believed to be able to cause water to flow from rocks, thus making him a fitting god for such a people. The architecture of the Puyupatamarka complex (above), *with its series of baths stepped down a hillside, suggests that it may have been a ceremonial center for the worship of water and earth.*

Personal hygiene was a high priority among the Incas. Stone conduits bordering city streets carried fresh mountain water to urban dwellers. The Spaniards were favorably impressed with the Incas' sanitation methods, but not enough to emulate them. Within a few years after the defeat of Atahualpa, these channels were clogged with refuse.

completely dependent on irrigation. In time, Chimu engineers became extraordinarily skillful in the design and construction of ever more complex canal systems.

The Chimu replaced the sand trenches of their predecessors with an intricate network of canals high up on the valley walls. These channels, which followed the contours of the land while maintaining a gently sloping gradient, were an innovative development requiring exact methods of surveying as well as elaborate structures able to carry the water across arroyos and canyons. The achievement is all the more remarkable for having been carried out with only the most primitive of implements. Some archaeologists believe that teams of 10 to 20 laborers working in tandem used stone and bronze tools to carve the rock. Boulders standing in the way were reduced in size by repeatedly heating them and then dashing them with icy water, so that flakes broke off. How the engineers chose the most likely slopes and best routes for canalization is unknown, although Charles R. Ortloff, a research associate at Chicago's Field Museum of Natural History, thinks that they used some sort of surveying device. This may have been a water-filled ceramic leveling bowl, balanced on a tripod, with a sighting tube running through it. Ortloff bases his claim on a bowl in an archaeological museum in Peru that may have served such a function.

Whatever the methods used, the results are impressive. One such project, the Intervalley Canal between the Moche and Chicama river valleys, stretched more than 45 miles. It spanned intervening gullies by means of landfill and aqueducts, cut across the intervalley divide, and finally spewed its contents into feeder canals above Chan Chan. Throughout its length the gradient and channel width had been exquisitely calculated by the Chimu hydraulic engineers to maintain a steady but rapid flow, with stone sluice gates allowing the amount drained off into croplands along its route to be rigorously determined. So vital was this water supply to Chimor that—or so oral history has it—Topa Inca Yupanqui had merely to cut it off, and the Chimu king surrendered. The Incas understood well that control of water meant power; they too were a hydraulic society.

The system of raised fields in the Lake Titicaca basin—called waru waru *or ca-mellones—is even today thought by some local inhabitants to have been constructed by a venerated "first race," who dominated the region prior to the Incas.*

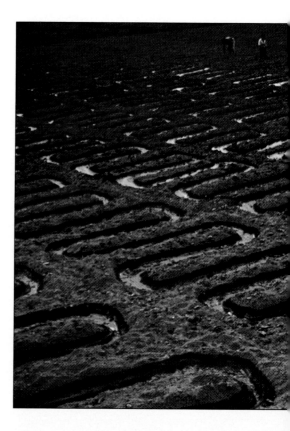

Although rain in the highlands fell in quantities that were more than adequate for crops native to the area, the cultivation of corn, originally a lowland plant, required a plentiful supply. To ensure that the corn would receive a steady flow of water, the Incas constructed a network of channels and canals, many miles long, carved out of the most difficult terrain with the simplest of tools. In at least one case, their attempts to control their resources extended to redirecting the course of a major waterway. At Pisac and Ollantaytambo, the mighty Urubamba River was straightened and canalized and its banks encased in stone to make more land available for farming and to reduce flooding. So impressed was Garcilaso by the Incas' canals that he could write of them, "One can compare them with the greatest works on earth and give them first place."

Waterworks projects were not an outgrowth of agricultural needs alone. They provided fresh water and waste disposal for many Inca towns. It was said that the engineers even directed the flow of thermal and regular springs so that some royals could enjoy the luxury of hot and cold running water. Reportedly, Pachacuti was responsible for the canalization of the two rivers that pass through Cuzco, a project undertaken to curtail seasonal flooding. Portions of this amazing piece of engineering, which could be seen into this century, are now covered by the city streets but are still functioning. Adept as they were at controlling water, the Incas were by no means

Water and earth intertwine in an ancient method of crop irrigation still in use in Peru's coastal areas and Ecuador's highlands. The cooperation essential to pursue major irrigation projects formed the basis of Andean civilization.

the first in the Andes to harness it for the good of society. In the early 1960s the remains of prehistoric raised fields for farming, with water channels adjacent to them, were discovered in Peru and Bolivia. Recent archaeological studies show that some date back to about 1000 BC and appear to have been abandoned before the Spaniards arrived. Raised fields have been found throughout much of South and Central America. One of the largest remnants of this form of agriculture, encompassing some 200,000 acres, lies on the plain surrounding the 3,100-square-mile Lake Titicaca. The lake's constant temperature of 51 degrees Fahrenheit helps moderate the harsh extremes of the puna climate, making cultivation possible despite the 12,500-foot altitude. But even with this advantage, if the local inhabitants had not resorted to the raised-field method of growing crops, their output would have been limited.

The raised fields were created by digging out parallel channels and heaping up the soil thereby removed in rectangular platforms, 12 to 30 feet wide, 30 to 300 feet long, and 3 feet high. The American geographer William Denevan, one of the first to study the raised fields, estimates that the entire Titicaca project would have required 145 million working days to construct. The efficiency of the design, however, made the work both desirable and necessary. The dredged-up earth was exceedingly fertile, and the platforms' elevation improved drainage and minimized the effects of flooding. The channels did much more than provide moisture during times of drought; they acted as heat sinks, absorbing the warmth of the sun during the day and releasing it at night when the air temperature plunged. An in-

GOLD AND SILVER: "SWEAT OF THE SUN, TEARS OF THE MOON"

No other peoples in all of pre-Columbian America had a greater repertoire of metallurgic techniques than the Chimu and the Incas. Indeed, in many ways the Peruvian craftsmen of that period were more sophisticated than their contemporaries in the Old World, even if their tools were not.

Using smooth, hard stones as both hammer and anvil, the metalsmiths pounded out the basic shape of the object from raw ingots. They then added their distinctive artistic touches by hammering the piece against a bas-relief template or etching it freehand with a stylus.

Although artisans sometimes employed closed- and open-mold casting, cold-hammering was the most common practice. To prevent the metal from becoming brittle as it was worked, it was sometimes subjected to a process called annealing, which means it was heated repeatedly to free it from internal stress and maintain pliability.

Graceful, wavelike motifs outline the border of this golden tumi, *or ceremonial knife, incised by a Chimu artisan who worked without benefit of steel engraving tools. Scholars are uncertain as to what the panel of anthropomorphic figures represents.*

sulating blanket was thus formed that helped both to keep the plants from freezing and to extend the growing season.

In a dramatic example of what is referred to today as experimental archaeology, which is a way of learning about the past by re-creating aspects of it to study, a team of agronomists and archaeologists led by Dr. Clark Erickson of the University of Pennsylvania duplicated the prehistoric raised beds and grew two of the crops that an analysis of ancient pollen recovered at the sites indicated might

This spectacular funerary mask of hammered, painted gold was created just to be buried with its owner. Almond-shaped eyes and rounded earplugs—worn by nobility—are common features of the art of the Kingdom of Chimor.

Silver objects (left) illustrate Chimu mastery of different metalworking techniques. The pieces were hammered, then soldered together. The musician fingers his panpipe with tattooed hands. The deer—an important food source—served as a burial offering.

have been cultivated 1,000 to 3,000 years ago—potatoes and quinoa. At harvest time, the yields from the raised beds surpassed everyone's wildest expectations. The normal potato crop in the region is 8 tons per acre. The first season, the return was more than double that. The following year, 1984, production reached 30 tons an acre.

With success like this, why were the fields abandoned? One theory proposed by Dr. Erickson suggests that the Titicaca area became depopulated as a result of disruption caused by the Inca conquest. Furthermore, by that time, the Incas were able to produce more than enough food for their expanding empire by using their improved terracing and irrigation methods, which often enabled them to harvest two crops a year.

The practicality and ingenuity of the Incas extended to all that they did, including metalworking, an old craft they raised to new heights. In 1928, some children playing near their small Peruvian

A bronze ceremonial tumi, *with its characteristic half-moon-shaped blade, tapers at the handle into the elongated neck of a llama. The motif is appropriate, since llamas were often ritualistically sacrificed and their entrails analyzed by priests to divine the future.*

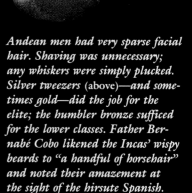

Andean men had very sparse facial hair. Shaving was unnecessary; any whiskers were simply plucked. Silver tweezers (above)—and sometimes gold—did the job for the elite; the humbler bronze sufficed for the lower classes. Father Bernabé Cobo likened the Incas' wispy beards to "a handful of horsehair" and noted their amazement at the sight of the hirsute Spanish.

village discovered a grave containing gold objects more than 2,000 years old. By the height of the Chimu dynasty in the 15th century, though, goldsmithing had developed from an individual pursuit to a highly organized and controlled personal industry serving the nobility. At the time of the Inca conquest of Chimor, the Chimu were acknowledged to be the Andes' most accomplished metalworkers.

The Chimu smiths and their Inca counterparts drew upon a wider repertoire of goldworking techniques than did any other Americans of their day. They cut pectorals and earplugs from hammered gold sheets, shaped cups and dishes around wooden templates, cast beads and statues, used gilding and plating, and closed loose edges with a type of soldering. They were adept at inlay, repoussé, and filigree. And as with all else they did, they managed to create masterpieces without, as Father Cobo said, "tongs, hammers, files, chisels, burins as well as the other implements used by our

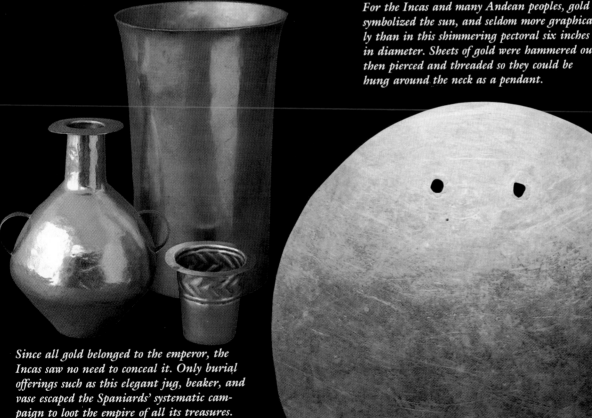

For the Incas and many Andean peoples, gold symbolized the sun, and seldom more graphically than in this shimmering pectoral six inches in diameter. Sheets of gold were hammered out, then pierced and threaded so they could be hung around the neck as a pendant.

Since all gold belonged to the emperor, the Incas saw no need to conceal it. Only burial offerings such as this elegant jug, beaker, and vase escaped the Spaniards' systematic campaign to loot the empire of all its treasures.

silversmiths." Another Spaniard, the historian Juan de Torquemada, wrote in 1613 that the smiths wrought objects of a beauty "greatly surpassing that of our Spanish jewelers because they could make birds whose heads, tongues, and wings could be made to move, and animals in whose paws they placed trinkets that seemed to dance."

Unlike silver, gold was, for the most part, not actually mined but rather panned or gathered in nugget or dust form. But where mines did exist, the labor required to extract ore was not deemed particularly onerous. Unlike later mines run by the Spaniards, whose relentless demands led to the death of many conscripted workers, the Inca operations were apparently models of enlightened management. The workday lasted from noon to sunset to prevent exhaustion in the oxygen-deprived air of the high altitudes; wives—who were allowed to stay with their husbands while they paid off their labor tax—cooked for their men, holidays were frequent, and each worker could return to his home after working his turn.

Bellows and blast furnaces were unknown; smelting temperatures of more than 1,000 degrees centigrade were reached in terracotta wind furnaces called *huairas*. In areas where a lack of wind prevented this type of furnace from being built, the workers, noted Garcilaso, "blasted by means of tubes of copper, the length of half a cubit, more or less, according as the furnace was large or small. The tubes were closed at one end, leaving one small hole through which the air could rush with more force. As many as 8, 10, or 12 of these were put together, and they went round the fire blowing with the tubes." The Incas' methods may have been rudimentary, but their output was extraordinary, and even those Spaniards whose task was to melt down the silver and gold objects looted from the empire must have felt some qualms about doing so. Not all production was artistic in nature; the Incas also manufactured practical items from tin, silver, copper, and lead, and from alloys of two or more metals.

As sophisticated and worldly-wise as the Europeans considered themselves to be, they were never able to adapt and adjust and operate productively in the harsh environment of Peru to the degree that the Incas and their predecessors had. After the conquest, the silver and gold began to run out, the terraces and irrigation canals were abandoned, the bridges were allowed to rot away, and the surviving buildings were neglected and left to decay. The legacy of the Incas, however, would live on in the spirit of their accomplishments and in their indomitable will in the face of adversity.

ARTISANS OF THE EMPIRE

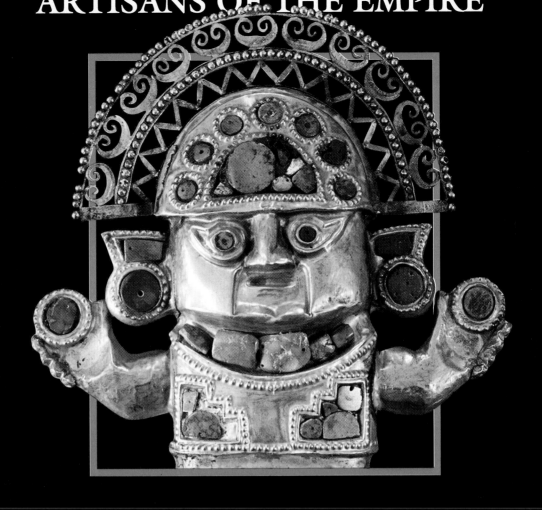

At the peak of its gilded glory in the 14th and 15th centuries, the Kingdom of Chimor spread 600 miles along the Peruvian coast. The Chimu, whose civilization reached full flower just prior to the ascendancy of the Incas, had reason to be proud of themselves. They were warriors who subdued all their potential rivals. They were city builders whose seaside capital of Chan Chan was most likely the biggest metropolis in pre-Columbian South America. They were farmers and engineers who built a large and ingenious network of canals to convey water from Andean streams to their parched and rainless homeland.

But most of all the Chimu were superb artisans who created objects of extraordinary intricacy and beauty from gold and silver; wood, shells, and bones; and feathers, cotton, and wool. Indeed, so numerous were the metalsmiths, carvers, weavers, and engravers of Chan Chan that archaeologists believe that out of an estimated population of 36,000 as many as 12,000 devoted themselves to arts production.

When archaeologists excavating the ruins of Chan Chan shifted their focus in the 1970s from the walled palaces of the Chimu kings to the barrios of the proletariat, they marveled at the craft remains they found in small houses and cramped workshops—ingots, hammers, bins stocked with cotton, unfinished textiles. The fact that so much of value had been left in the ruins suggested a hasty exit, probably at the time of the Inca conquest of the Chimu between 1465 and 1470. But where did the artisans go? The Incas knew a good thing when they saw it and brought the most talented of Chan Chan's citizens to their capital of Cuzco. Doubtless it was the hands of gifted Chimu designers, ironically, that produced many of the golden treasures that so dazzled and excited the conquistadors—and thus hastened the end of the Incas themselves.

THE GOLDEN CITY OF THE DEAD

The Chimu capital of Chan Chan resembled no place else. Where other cities had plazas and boulevards, Chan Chan's core was a succession of royal compounds archaeologists call *ciudadelas* (little cities) that lay concealed behind adobe walls up to 30 feet high and 2,000 feet long. Each consisted of a maze of corridors connecting storerooms, officelike chambers, courtyards, residential quarters, and burial mounds.

Archaeologists at first thought that the ciudadelas segregated the population socially or occupationally, but later research seems to indicate that each compound was in fact a palace. When a king died, he was probably laid to rest in his own abode, beside an ample selection of worldly goods and dozens, perhaps hundreds, of young female sacrificial victims. The property, in turn, passed to his relations, while his successor took up residence in a new compound.

Smaller compounds adjoining the ciudadelas, probably the homes of nobles and high-ranking bureaucrats, formed a buffer between the royal palaces and the barrio dwellings of the commoners. The society that emerges from the archaeological record was urban, well organized, materialistic, theocratic (kings were thought to be divine), and aggressive. But its strange, inward-looking capital, with its walls-within-walls palaces that ultimately became royal mausoleums, was also, even in its own time, a city of the dead.

Chan Chan's urban sprawl is evident in this photograph of a portion of its 10-square-mile expanse and in the schematic map (below) of the city's core area. The map shows locations of the walled ciudadelas, or royal compounds (gold), *the barrios, or artisans' quarters* (brown), *and sunken gardens* (light gold), *and also identifies important structures within the compound seen in the foreground of the photograph. The sprawling ciudadelas occupied about a quarter of Chan Chan. Large gardens, like the greenish rectangle in the picture, were placed below ground level so that plants could draw directly on the water table. Regrettably for the Chimu, the plots did not produce enough food for the citizenry. More crops were planted in outlying fields irrigated by canals. The Incas conquered the Chimu by cutting off Chan Chan's water supply.*

1 Burial mound
2 Sunken garden
3 Ceremonial plazas
4 Audiencias, or reception areas
5 Large storage area for prestige goods

HUMBLE MUD TRANSFORMED INTO HIGH ART

Art was everywhere in Chimor—on clothing and jewelry, on knives and litters and household utensils, and most of all on the walls. Elaborate, often geometrical friezes covered walls at the great Chan Chan palaces. In a city of straight lines and right angles the Chimu filled the vast adobe surfaces around them with friezes fashioned three different ways—by carving directly in the wet clay, by pressing the clay into large forms, and by molding the material in relief planes in a technique similar to embossing. Although everything in Chan Chan today is pale ocher like the surrounding earth, the friezes, most of which had maritime themes, were originally plastered and in some cases brightly painted. Surviving designs are symmetrical and stylized, often interspersing a geometric pattern with depictions of mammals, birds, fish, and mythical creatures. They look like textile patterns transposed to adobe, which they might well have been.

Though recognizing the Chimu as master architects, archaeologists wondered why Chan Chan's walls were built in sections that had no structural or artistic rationale. One expert, combining the wall segments with the Chimu policy of labor as taxation, theorizes that a single unit of adobe wall represented the production of one work crew in a given time period. However they were made, Chan Chan's mud walls were built to last. Generally about 13 feet wide at the base and tapering to 4 to 5 feet at the top, they have withstood 600 to 800 years of sporadic earthquakes without disappearing.

The restored friezes on the Huaca del Dragon (above), a sacred site outside Chan Chan, portray arched, double-headed serpents and other mythical as well as real creatures. The design at the near end shows a clash of mythic figures surrounded by masked men bearing spears. The structure was probably dedicated to the moon goddess, Si, who, rather than the sun god, was worshiped as the supreme deity by the Chimu because of her power over the sea, storms, and crops.

These bas-relief friezes in the Ciudadela Velarde have sea themes. The first depicts a small reed boat called a caballito *(little horse) that has persisted in the area to the present day. On the boat's prow sits a cormorant. The second frieze incorporates fish, squid, and other marine life still to be found in local waters.*

Diamond-shaped carvings line the wall of this now roofless audiencia, *or receiving room, in a Chan Chan palace. The niches and bins are thought to be either for the display of precious objects or for storage. The walls' rounded edges are the result of centuries of weathering.*

AN OYSTER AS REVERED AS GOLD

An old legend tells of the first king of a province north of Chan Chan eventually conquered by the Chimu. The story goes that he arrived by sea, bringing with him wives, concubines, attendants, and eight deputies, one of whom was charged with scattering before him a carpet of red dust produced from spiny oyster shells. The species *(below)*, called *spondylus,* was held in high esteem in Chimor. Archaeologists found the reddish shells of the mollusk—whole, in pieces, and crushed to powder—at every royal burial site. One cache of *spondylus* was discovered interred alone, as if the shells themselves were royalty. But the most remarkable fact about this mollusk is that it is native not to Peruvian waters but to the warmer seas off Ecuador.

The question of why the *spondylus* was so prized remains a riddle. One scholar speculates that its importance is linked with El Niño storms that periodically bring catastrophic floods to the Peruvian coast. By this theory the oysters move south in the warm El Niño currents that kill most of the indigenous cold-water fish. They were thus an omen of death—and, perhaps, a totem to be venerated.

The intricate neckpiece above, which may have been worn by a Chimu king, combines vivid spondylus *and mussel shells with jet and a mother-of-pearl fringe. Despite its numerous beads, it was made without a fabric backing, and is held together instead with cotton thread.*

Spiny outside, shells of the mollusk spondylus *reveal their colorful interior. When Pizarro's men captured a balsa raft in their first contact with the Incas, they found shells like these in its cargo.*

116

In a society without wheeled vehicles, the wondrously decorated wooden litter below found near Chan Chan was the equivalent of a royal limousine. The gold, turquoise, shells, and wooden carvings artfully added to the back of the litter, seen here, depict masked and bewigged figures representing a dignitary flanked by two attendants in an audiencia.

The spondylus-and-stone mosaic inlaid on the wooden bowl (above) illustrates how the shells were gathered. The detail work shows a boat with a cabin, the divers below, boatmen holding their lifelines, and depictions of the shell itself.

Made from the feathers of a blue-and-yellow macaw like the one at left, this tunic features a pattern of lordly pelicans borne on litters by lesser birds. Chimu featherworkers were partial to two other species of macaws—the scarlet and the red-and-green—along with Muscovy ducks and paradise tanagers.

RESPLENDENT RAIMENT FOR THE CHOSEN FEW

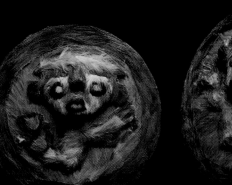

These wood-and-feather earplugs blend the finely chopped plumes of macaws (red and yellow), parrots (green), and tanagers or honeycreepers (purple). The wooden figures have been carved so that they are raised from the surface as in relief.

Chimu workshops were team enterprises. Archaeologists sifting through the dust of 600-year-old barrios frequently found implements for metalsmithing in the same small rooms with spindles and woodworking tools, suggesting a division of labor that doubtless would have facilitated the creation of items like clothing adorned with feathers and gold, or wooden pieces inlaid with stones and shells.

While the everyday outfit for men was a tunic and loincloth, and for women a horizontally wrapped dress, on ceremonial occasions the Chan Chan nobles turned out in brilliantly colored feathers or in garments of luxurious alpaca and vicuna wool. Since wool came from the highlands, and feathers from the macaws, parrots, and other birds of the Amazon basin, obtaining them demanded a far-reaching trade network. The wool arrived at the manufacturing nexus at Chan Chan already spun and dyed; there it was woven into richly patterned cloth.

Curiously, Chimu textile goods were found to be more widely dispersed in Peru after the Inca conquest of Chimor than before. The most likely explanation: The Incas collected textiles as taxes and then recirculated them as rewards or payment.

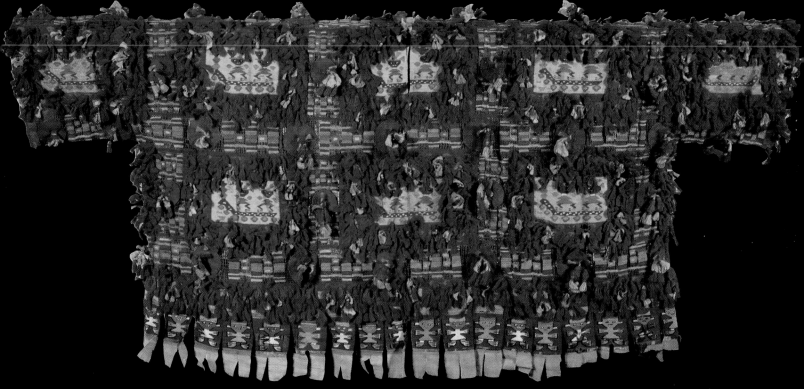

The tassels and tapestry weave on this tunic are probably dyed alpaca wool. Since wool had to be imported, it was used sparingly, often in tapestry bands or as embroidery on cotton. The design here is the familiar Chimu motif of two men in a boat. The slits on the fringe were not cut but woven in; many Andean peoples deemed cutting fabric a sacrilege.

GLITTERING GARB THAT PROCLAIMED KINGSHIP

For centuries, Andean peoples had been plucking gold from their streams and digging it out of their mountains. By Chimu times gold mining was a major industry; one account estimates that 6,000 men toiled in the royal mines. The ore was smelted in hillside "wind furnaces," where air blowing through apertures in chimneys raised the temperature of the fires; or by lung power, with miners blowing through tubes to fan the smelters' flames. Shipped to Chan Chan in ingots, the metal was pounded into sheets with small stone hammers and fashioned into implements, decorative pieces, and ornaments for glittering garments like those shown here, using a variety of sophisticated methods including welding and soldering.

The Chimu valued gold not as wealth—they had no coinage—but as a symbol of power and prestige. With them, as with the Incas, none but the elite could garb themselves in gold. The lords of Chimu drank from golden goblets, combed their hair with golden combs, and plucked their whiskers with golden tweezers. To the Chimu, it appears, gold was treasured more as an idea than as a fact, as an essence rather than as an object. For them, the glow of gold was a luster that shone from within, an expression of royal power.

Spangled with 18-carat gold platelets, this ceremonial robe dates from the conquest of Chimor by the Incas. It may have draped the shoulders of a Chimu king or been specially created for an Inca ruler. Small masks are sewn into the geometrically patterned central band with characteristic Chimu symmetry.

The gold pieces on this shirt depict shells, frogs, and human faces along with geometric shapes that may have held emblematic meaning. Apparently, property in Chimu society was regarded as a divine right reserved for the nobility. Theft of such a valuable shirt would thus have been seen as a crime both religious and civil, meriting the death of not only the culprit but also his parents and siblings.

The bag at right, with layers of quadrangular gold disks covering its cloth base, was probably a gilded fashion accessory for a Chimu noble. Similar bags were employed by the Incas for holding coca leaves, the mildly narcotic stimulant that members of the Chimu nobility, in keeping with their status, may have used.

LIVES OF HARD WORK AND JOYOUS PLAY

hen the Avenida Progreso, the coastal highway that wends east of Lima, Peru, was being constructed, laborers cut through a massive burial mound at the city's borders, exposing pre-Columbian graves and their contents—bits of pottery, wooden implements, mummy wrappings, bones, and skulls to which patches of dried skin and clumps of hair were still attached. To the inhabitants of Lima this would not have been regarded as a particularly unusual occurrence, since the grounds of many of their modern homes conceal such grim mementos and, as one observer wrote, "In cultivating their flower gardens, the residents are as likely to turn up skulls as stones."

Graveyards overflowing with ancient human remains abound between the Andes and the Pacific coast, from Ecuador to Chile, in the lands that once were provinces of the Inca empire. In the warm, dry coastal area, mummy bundles—bodies wound in yards of cloth—have been naturally preserved beneath the sands. Plundering the sites has provided a tidy income for generations of professional grave-robbers, known as *huaqueros*. Looking for relics, these thieves have greedily ravaged thousands of cemeteries, leaving behind fields of bones and desiccated bodies.

So it could hardly have seemed consequential to inhabitants of the modern city of Ancón, 20 miles north of Lima, when, in 1976,

Desecrated by hua-queros—*local grave-robbers—for whatever valuables it contained, this pre-Inca cemetery near Lima bears mute witness to the once-glorious past—and to the damage inflicted on it by treasure hunters.*

on the outskirts of their city, some unauthorized bulldozing blundered on mummified remains dating back to the century of Inca supremacy. It was merely the corpse of an unidentifiable woman, swathed in four layers of cloth wrappings together with her seemingly worthless possessions. The find might have been negligible, considering that during the past five decades, more than 2,000 mummy bundles had been uncovered in this region alone.

For Peruvian archaeologists, however, that casual discovery marked a valuable milestone in antiquarian research. The ransacking of ruins by huaqueros had contributed more than a million artifacts to the world's museums and private collections. But while producing abundant evidence of the diversity of the old culture, such scavenging had divorced the objects from their owners.

Now, however, archaeologists had access to a perfectly preserved mummy bundle, and they set about examining it with scientific care, meticulously unraveling it and photographing and recording each step of the process. Ultimately, the style of the bundle and of the numerous artifacts within it yielded a wealth of information about a woman of modest means who had lived some time between AD 1476 and 1532 *(pages 152-153)*.

The woman of Ancón—as she has come to be known—had been interred after long and laborious preparation and the donation of many gifts, and her burial reflected the high esteem accorded someone who had toiled with great industry and skill. This was the centuries-old way of Andean peoples—to find virtue and satisfaction in meaningful labor and to commemorate it in death. As Pedro Cieza de León reported immediately after the Spanish conquest: "No one who was lazy or tried to live by the work of others was tolerated; everyone had to work."

The Incas were quick to take advantage of this pervasive work ethic. Their imperial ambitions demanded that there be a class of citizens below the nobility, willing and able to wrest from the mountains and deserts the means to feed not only themselves but also a religious establishment that consumed enormous resources and an upper caste bent on creating a high culture. In the Andean peoples, the Incas had a vigorous peasantry that proved a worthy match for their requirements. In the details of their lives, these industrious folk revealed how creatively they had adapted to the hardships of their

Dr. Karen Stothert (left) *and a team from the National Institute of Culture in Lima assiduously photograph and catalog the contents of a mummy bundle they have just unwrapped. Scraps of cloth—here being gingerly placed in bags for later analysis—and the wood and rope pieces of a loom* (bottom, center) *buried with these remains of a wellborn but apparently not wealthy woman have provided archaeologists with much data on everyday life in the Inca empire.*

varied environments, from the type of shoes they wore to the way they led their communal existence.

At the same time that they imposed a heavy work load on their subjects, the Incas—in seeming contradiction to their fundamental purpose—reduced the productivity of the peasants by devoting an inordinate amount of time and resources to great festivals, religious rituals, and public ceremonies. Approximately a third of the year was given over to these events. The largesse expended on them, however, was not lavished in vain; these celebrations forged links between the empire and the citizenry that made bearable the heavy demands of the Sapa Inca.

In this work-intensive society, laws rigidly regulated lives. They directed where people might live, what crops they might grow, how they might dress, even whom they might marry. An examination of these laws, as recorded by early Spanish chroniclers, as well as study of the surviving artifacts, has made it possible for scholars to reconstruct in minute detail the lifestyle of the common citizen of Tahuantinsuyu.

The dual sources of psychological support for the peasants in their daily round of endless tasks were the family and the *ayllu,* a patrilineal community consisting of a number of extended families living near one another and working collectively. There might be several ayllus in a large farm settlement, each occupying a block of dwellings surrounded by a walled-off area, each having its own revered ancestors, and each keeping to its designated section at festivals in the local village plaza.

The Incas superimposed on the ayllus their decimal-based bureaucratic organization of households into economic units of tens, hundreds, and thousands, each controlled by a curaca, the official who, among other duties, collected the taxes that the people paid in

125

the form of agricultural produce and cloth. But for the ordinary family it was the ayllu that mattered, not the decimal unit to which the members happened to belong.

Every adult male within an ayllu, upon marriage, received from the Sapa Inca an allotment of land, or *topo,* that was just large enough to support himself and his wife. The size of the topo varied according to the fertility of the region, but if, for example, a topo measured two acres, then, according to the chronicler Garcilaso de la Vega, it was increased by a further two acres for each son the couple had to support, and by one-half acre for each daughter. As holder of a topo, the newly wed male was automatically registered as a *puric,* a tax-paying head of a household who was duly bound also to work on state lands and on property belonging to the religious establishment.

Modern scholars have pondered the role of the puric's wife in this setup. The ethnohistorian Irene Silverblatt has made much of the fact that the topo was allotted to a man only if he was married. She has suggested that although the land was formally presented to the husband, it was, in actuality, given to man and wife as a unit, indicating their complementary and thus equal share of the tax burden.

But who, in fact, worked harder? Some ethnohistorians have concluded that the plebeian wife, with small children, bore the brunt of the toil. Indeed, the Spanish conquistadors saw women as being virtually slaves of their husbands, condemned to a life of drudgery. It would be misleading, however, to judge the role of Andean women by the standards of the Spaniards, who equated hard physical labor with inferior status. Just as Father Bernabé Cobo saw these peasant women as "slaves," so the part-Andean chronicler, Felipe Huaman Poma de Ayala, whose mother was an Inca, viewed Spanish women as indolent and immoral because they remained idle even when they were able-bodied. Within Andean culture, men and women regarded their working roles as mutually supportive and, for survival, necessarily so.

Within the ayllu, a sense of solidarity prevailed. The men got together to build the houses for newlyweds; and

Crafted by a skillful Chimu potter from the northern coastal region of the Incas' realm, this foot-long ceramic vessel depicts a fisherman with his lobster pot and catch. Images of traditional life are rare; Inca artisans generally eschewed realism and the human figure, concentrating instead on intricate geometric designs.

126

when one of them was called to serve out his mit'a, which might involve a stint in the army or on a public-works force, those who stayed behind took care of his topo on his family's behalf. At the time of the spring planting, when the ecclesiastical lands were plowed first, the men and women worked facing one another, chanting in time. The men turned up the soil with the *taclla,* a foot plow consisting of a pole about six feet long, with a footrest jutting out above its point of fire-hardened wood or bronze. The women followed behind, using a *lampa,* a simple hoe with a wide, chisel-shaped bronze blade, to break up the clods.

Nothing, of course, was more important to the ayllu than the success of each year's harvest. Throughout the empire the initial breaking of the soil was undertaken with great ceremony, the local dignitary making the first cut. The emperor and his court often participated on his own estates near Cuzco, where he used a gold-tipped taclla to initiate the planting. But Father Cobo observed that the Sapa Inca "soon stopped working, and after him the other officials and nobles stopped also, and sat down with the king to their banquets and festivals, which were especially notable on such days." After this symbolic gesture, and the festival that followed, the rest of the work would be left to the commoners. When they had finished preparing the property of the religious establishment, they would plow and sow the lands of the state, leaving their own allotments to be worked last of all.

Corn, the color of the sun, was by far the most valued crop and the food judged most fit for offering to the gods. But the peasants grew an enormous range of other plants—various beans and squashes, chili peppers, manioc, avocados, peanuts, gourds, cotton, coca, quinoa, a highland grain, and, not least of all, potatoes, of which there were more than 220 varieties. Such an assortment of food plants—some more suitable to one environment than another—involved planting and harvesting at different times of the year. As if caring for the fields was not enough, the peasants had to attend to myriad other tasks from fetching water, grinding corn, and brewing *chicha,* a beer usually made with a corn base, to weaving baskets and turning out earthenware jars used for cooking, serving, and storing

Doing double duty, a peasant woman nurses her baby while carrying a large arybalto, *or* chicha *jug, strapped to her shoulders. The motif of this ceremonial vessel accurately illustrates the arduous lot of commoners in Peru's rugged, demanding environment; no respite from the usual workaday tasks was taken, not even by new mothers.*

127

food. And in addition to all these chores, there was still the spinning and weaving of cloth to be done, for the family's needs and for the state.

While the Incas demanded that everyone work, they adjusted the rules to take into account the capacity or condition of the worker. The sick and the disabled were not required to support themselves. They were fed and clothed from the government storehouses, and only allotted duties suited to their physical condition. At the same time, however, the ever-pragmatic Inca regime ensured that the handicapped did not hold back any able-bodied citizen from gainful employment through their special needs. By law, a person with a major disability could only marry someone with a like disability—the blind to the blind, the deaf to the deaf, hunchbacks to hunchbacks, and dwarfs to dwarfs.

The elderly also received special consideration. A person was judged to have reached old age at around fifty. No longer qualified as fully able-bodied workers, those of advanced years were exempt from mit'a service and freed from taxation. No one was ever completely retired, however. For as long as possible the elderly were expected to undertake light duties, such as gathering brushwood, baby-sitting, preparing food and chicha, twisting ropes, and assisting at harvesttime.

Although women worked in the fields and cared for the children, they still were expected to weave. The woman of Ancón may have been a prodigious weaver; in any case, she was buried with a vast amount of cloth. There were about 17 yards of fabric in her wrappings alone, representing, by one scholarly estimate, more than 850 hours put in on spindle and loom. Two wicker workbaskets in her mummy bundle were packed with the implements and materials she had used. Women, including even noble Inca ladies, were forever spinning—as they walked and talked, as they kept an eye on their youngsters, as they watched over their cooking.

Men, too, were known to weave, although they more commonly took care of a family's apparel needs by cobbling sandals of untanned leather from the thick hide on the neck of the llama, tying their handiwork with woolen cords. Father Cobo describes a typical sandal as having a "sole which was shorter than the length of the foot, so that their toes extend out beyond the end of the sole, permitting them to grip with their toes when they are climbing uphill."

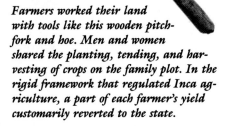

Farmers worked their land with tools like this wooden pitchfork and hoe. Men and women shared the planting, tending, and harvesting of crops on the family plot. In the rigid framework that regulated Inca agriculture, a part of each farmer's yield customarily reverted to the state.

In Inca society there was no opportunity to be lazy. Even childbearing women got little respite from the daily grind. The mother-to-be might be excused from agricultural work during the advanced stages of pregnancy, but otherwise she was expected to carry out all her household chores for as long as was physically possible. Not that the arrival of a child was trivialized. On the contrary, it was joyfully celebrated. From the Inca viewpoint, children were valued as future additions to the work force. Abortion, therefore—accomplished by beatings, fetal massages, and drugs—was, under the laws of the empire, a capital offense for both the mother and anyone who assisted her in the crime.

It was customary for the expectant mother to pray for safe delivery, and for the father to do his part to assure a successful outcome by fasting while she was in labor. But otherwise, childbirth was seen as a natural function to be conducted with a minimum of fuss. Although there were no midwives, mothers of twins were seen as having special expertise and sometimes assisted other mothers as they gave birth. More often, a peasant woman delivered her baby unaided, then bathed the newborn and herself in the nearest stream. Wherever she went, she would carry the infant bundled in a backpack tied across her chest with a shawl.

Every infant was breast-fed for as long as possible. Once the child had been weaned, its parents observed the ceremony called *rutuchicoy,* a feast attended by relations and friends. Here, the senior male relative would cut off a lock of the youngster's hair. Other guests followed suit, and each presented the child with a gift, usually cloth-

In this drawing, a woman at the time of the Incas harvests potatoes with a hoe similar to the example shown on the opposite page, while a man turns the soil with a taclla, *or foot plow. With no large draft animals available, peasants used ordinary wooden tacllas to till their land. The ornate ceremonial taclla replica at right bears a jug for* chicha *as well as an ear of corn, together indicating the Incas' high regard for the grain that was a source of both food and drink.*

ing or wool. The fingernails were also trimmed, and the nail and hair cuttings were carefully preserved by the family.

Until this point in his or her life, the child had simply been called *wawa,* or baby. Now, at the rutuchicoy, the infant was given a provisional name recalling the circumstances or place of its birth— for example, Thunderstorm, or Fine Sand. This name would be used throughout childhood, with a permanent name bestowed at puberty. At that time a boy would be named for an animal or a quality associated with an animal—Puma, for example, or Dragon, Snake, Hawk, or perhaps Brave, Honorable, or Happy. Girls were given names such as Star, Halo, Coca, Gold, or called after a flower.

Boys attained maturity at about 14, celebrated by another feast, the *huarachicoy.* This was an elaborate community affair at which each initiate received his first *huara,* or loincloth, the insignia of manhood, spun and woven by his mother. For girls, puberty rites involved only family and friends in a two-day event known as a *quicochicoy.* It was celebrated after a girl's first menstruation, at which time she began three days of fasting and confinement while her mother busied herself weaving her daughter a new outfit. On the fourth day, freshly bathed, dressed in handsome clothes, and crowned with braided hair, the young woman emerged to greet her guests. Each presented her with a gift, and the senior male relative chose her permanent name and lectured her on her future conduct and the need to obey her parents at all times.

Unlike the sons of nobles and curacas, the children of commoners received no formal edu-

A newborn rests in snug comfort, securely strapped to a quirau, *or cradle. Babies were carried this way until they were able to keep up with their mothers in their daily activities. Inca parents of all castes tutored their children from an early age in the vocational pursuits that, more than any other element, would define the remainder of their lives.*

cation. As one Inca ruler declared: "It is not right that the children of plebeians should be taught knowledge that is only suitable for nobles, lest the lower classes rise up and grow arrogant and bring down the republic. It is enough that they learn the trades of their fathers, for governing is no matter for them."

This judgment was probably accepted without question by ordinary people who needed to pass on to their offspring their basic skills and introduce them into the work force as early as possible. Education, to them, meant simply the lessons children got from their parents as they assisted them in daily tasks. To be sure, youngsters had some toys and diversions. They played at *pisqoynyo* (whipping tops) and games of chance involving the throwing of counters consisting of readily available potsherds. But nothing mattered more in their lives than learning the obligatory skills and crafts.

Even here the state had a say. The Incas imposed a womb-to-tomb uniformity over jobs by dividing all subjects into 12 categories according to age and sex. Within these every man, woman, and child, from five years old on, had designated tasks to fulfill. In the early years, girls assisted in minding babies and making chicha, fetching water and fodder, and weeding. Young boys looked after the animals and shooed birds away from crops.

Girls began weaving as early as possible. Between the ages of 9 and 12, they were also responsible for the gathering of medicinal and culinary herbs and plants used in making dyes for textiles. In adolescence, some worked as shepherdesses, but most remained at home, weaving and performing household tasks. And before long it was the decreed time for them to marry.

In marriage, as in education, two standards applied, one for the aristocrat and one for the ordinary citizen. While polygamy prevailed among the upper classes, monogamy was the rule for virtually every male commoner, since the state entrusted him with only enough land to support two adults and their offspring. By the same token, long-term bachelorhood was untenable, for a male had to marry to obtain a topo—in effect, to support himself. Accordingly, the great majority of young men were supposed to wed by the age of twenty-five. For girls, the prescribed period for acquiring a husband was between 16 and twenty.

Trial marriages were not unusual in many areas. A child born during a trial marriage that failed might remain with the mother and her family. But no stigma was attached to the unmarried mother. In stark contrast to Spanish beliefs, virginity was not a prized condition. Indeed, Father Cobo wrote that "virginity was regarded as a drawback for the woman, for the Indians held that only those remained virgins who had not learned to make themselves loved by someone." His contention is supported by stories told by other chroniclers, including one in which a husband chastised his wife for not having had any lovers before their marriage.

Leaving nothing to chance, the ever-efficient state set aside one specific time in the year for registering betrothals in a collective, nonreligious ceremony. On the appointed day, in the plaza of every town and village, young men and women who had reached the prescribed marital age assembled in two lines before an Inca official, usually the local curaca. Each young man was then invited to declare the bride of his choice. In all likelihood, this pairing off was already a *fait accompli,* approved by the respective parents. If a male adult of 25 or older could not decide for himself, the presiding curaca had it within his power to choose a bride for him. He could also adjudicate in any dispute over a woman coveted by more than one man.

Only a numerical imbalance between the sexes—partially brought about by the loss of men in frequent warfare—disturbed the neatness of the system. The surplus of women was to a degree offset by the selection of girls for education in the provincial *Acllahuasi,* the House of the Chosen Women. Other women, including widows, became domestic servants, or were employed in making pottery and, especially, cloth.

Cloth figured importantly in Inca society. Valued in its own right as a product of intensive labor, it also set apart the classes. For the common man, basic wear consisted of a plain knee-length, sleeveless tunic of cotton or rough wool worn over a loincloth, and the *yacolla,* a large rectangular cloak with two corners knotted on the

Tupu *pins like these were used to fasten the woolen cloak worn around the shoulders and also served as an Andean woman's principal item of jewelry. Most were five or six inches long, and their intricacy varied greatly according to the owner's social status. The plain bronze tupu belonged to a commoner, while the more elaborate gold example most certainly adorned the mantle of a noblewoman.*

132

chest or one shoulder. The woman of Ancón was buried in a typical female garment, similar to a male tunic except that it fell to the ankles; she would have worn it with a sash, an optional feature for the male. Over their shoulders women draped a *lliclla*, a kind of shawl fastened with a large-headed, decorative metal pin, the *tupu*.

As was noted earlier, only Inca nobles could wear *cumbi,* by grade the finest cloth. Cumbi was finished on both sides and woven in many colors by professional weavers and the chosen women. Yet the peasants were not to be outdone; they wove decorative patterns into their coarser fabrics, sometimes combining the natural hues of cotton that they had learned how to grow in shades of brown, tan, beige, and gray. For other clothing, they created colorful designs using a spectrum of dyes made of substances from nature.

The workbasket of the woman of Ancón, for example, contained skeins of brightly dyed blue, maroon, and yellow threads, and organic and mineral substances probably used for dyeing materials. While the state mandated the people's dress, the simplicity of their housing no doubt arose more from custom and necessity than from government control. Depending on climate and the construction materials available, building styles varied greatly from one region to another. In provinces east of the Andes, which had extremely hot temperatures and an abundance of trees, dwellings were large, airy, and made of wood. On coastal plains, where it never rains, rectangular huts—some of earth and adobe, others of cane interwoven with reeds—could have flat roofs, covered by reeds or branches. In the cold, wind-swept highlands, dwellings were of rough

This ceramic vessel illustrates a prevalent form of Inca footwear. Sandals were made from llama hide, plaited wool, or the durable fibers of the aloe plant. In some cases, moccasins were worn.

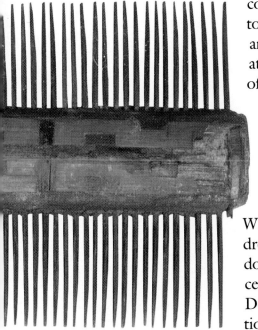

Combs figured importantly in the daily grooming ritual, since Inca women of every social stratum wore their hair long. Two-sided combs, such as the one shown here, were the most common type and were made of cactus spines or long thorns that were laid between two flat pieces of wood, then bound tightly together with brightly colored thread.

stone and mud, with roofs of straw. At the center of these one-room, windowless structures usually stood a small clay oven, fueled with dried llama dung or branches from bushes or scrub. Smoke escaped through the thatch. A few niches might serve as cupboards for household utensils.

Neither Incas nor their subjects possessed furniture of any kind, with the exception of the *duho,* the low stool whose use was the prerogative of the Sapa Inca and those nobles and curacas to whom he extended the privilege. As Father Cobo described the stool, it was usually carved from one piece of wood in the shape of an animal "with short legs, lowered head, and the tail high."

Peasant families rarely gathered in their dark shelters until after nightfall, or when it was raining heavily or bitterly cold. As long

The walls of the military garrison at Tambo Colorado reflect the basic floor plan that was found in all Inca residential construction—the cancha. *At right, a clay model—sculpted as a religious offering—shows the same layout as it applies to a one-family compound.*

as the weather permitted it, they took their meals in the open air; indeed, under Pachacuti, eating outdoors became law. At bedtime, the family stretched out on the floor of the hut, sometimes on a little straw. Parents and children slept together under coarse woolen blankets known as *chusi*, still wearing most of their day clothes, husband and wife shedding only their cloaks.

Two meals a day were eaten, one soon after dawn and the other an hour or two before sunset. The food was cooked in earthenware pots placed on several round openings cut in the top of the stove. At mealtimes, the family squatted or sat on the ground. Father Cobo, having observed one couple, reported their sitting posture as an extremely comfortable one: "With their feet together, they bend their legs as much as they can; their knees come up so far as to almost touch their chins. On sitting they drop their tunics down to their feet so that the whole body fits into the tunic, except for their heads." The tunic, pulled tight, held the legs.

Most commonly, meals consisted of boiled or roasted corn and either potatoes or quinoa, a tiny grain that puffed up in cooking like barley. These formed the base of soups and stews to which a variety of beans and herbs such as hot chilies might be added. It was not unknown for soups to be further flavored by the addition of small birds, frogs, and certain edible worms. This corn-dominated diet was supplemented by an enormous range of tubers and fruits, which varied from region to region.

Fish was, of course, plentiful on the coast and around Lake Titicaca. But in most highland areas, the main and only regular source of meat was the guinea pig, an animal that lived and multiplied with the family and, when roasted, provided delicious fare. In some areas ducks were raised for food, and in Huanca province dogs were eaten, a practice much despised elsewhere. Outside a peasant dwelling, an enclosure might hold a few llamas. Herds of these animals provided the nobility with good, mutton-flavored meat. But for the ordinary person, such food was a luxury to be enjoyed only when an animal had ceased being of use. As a beast of burden and a source of wool, llamas were too valuable to waste as food. When they were eaten, often the meat was cut into thin strips, dried by exposure to the sun and frost, then pounded between two stones to flatten and tenderize it. All meat preserved this way was known as *charqui*.

The peasants would not drink chicha from their tumblers until after eating. This cloudy beer, consumed every day in moderation and in great quantities at festival time, could be produced from a number of cultivated plants other than corn, including quinoa and oca. If the corn was old, the pulp needed to be chewed; the saliva broke down the starch into sugar that facilitated fermentation. The ensuing paste was spat out into jars of warm water, which were sealed and then buried to maintain a constant degree of warmth. After a day or two, the chicha was ready for drinking. This time-consuming preparation process could be accomplished sitting down and required no physical strength. It was an activity especially suited to the old and infirm, and the Incas, making sure that no one would be completely idle, officially specified it as such.

Young, able-bodied women spent a great deal of their time preserving food for later consumption. Corn and quinoa were ground into flour on a flat stone slab with a long, crescent-shaped stone, which was rocked from side to side to crush the grain. In the highlands, women produced dehydrated potatoes, or *chuño,* a product that would keep for many months. The making of chuño was usually undertaken in June, when the Andean days are warm and the night temperatures, at 12,000 feet, fall below freezing. The potatoes were laid out on the ground to freeze so that the cell walls would rupture, then allowed to thaw in the morning sun. At noon, they would be arranged in small heaps and trodden upon with bare feet to squeeze out the juices. This process was repeated several times to remove as much moisture as possible. After a thorough rinsing to eliminate any bitter taste, the pulp was allowed to dehydrate. Chuño and other dried foods were stored in earthenware jars or bins made from cornstalks.

The dwellings of purics were hives of activity. Since they were in effect production units, these factory-like houses had to be correctly maintained and managed. To assure that they would be,

VARIED FARE SUITED TO INCA NEEDS

Long before the Incas rose to dominance, settlement of Peru's bleak, forbidding highlands had been made possible in large part by the potato—an indigenous tuber that has since become a staple crop throughout the world. Thriving at altitudes of almost three miles, hardy and frost resistant, potatoes—and oca, a type of yam—could be mashed, dried, and stored in dehydrated form.

Early inhabitants had also transplanted corn from the lower altitudes along the coast to sheltered, terraced slopes in the Andes prior to the arrival of the Incas. As they enlarged their domain, the Incas devoted energy and resources to bringing more land under cultivation and increased yields of this adaptable, utilitarian crop. The new masters of the Andes had to feed not only their subjects but also a standing army that kept

Rendered in bronze, these ears of corn may have been a reminder of corn's ceremonial link to the sun and the Inca belief that nobles and virtuous people merged with the sun after death. The contents of the basket (right) found in the mummy bundle of the woman of Ancón (page 152) includes corn, beans, cotton, and fruit. The offerings probably stood for new life, fertility, and reproduction.

A fish-shaped ceremonial vessel dates from around AD 1500. An important source of protein to the peoples of the coast and the region around Lake Titicaca, fish were a natural subject for the artisan.

order in the territories.

One of the Incas' greatest achievements was eliminating the threat of famine throughout their empire. They earned loyalty from conquered tribes by establishing stockpiles and efficient distribution of food in times of need. In fact, during the Incas' reign, the population of the Andes enjoyed a nourishing, varied diet. The extensive road network and efficient organization the Incas created permitted highland crops to be bartered for squashes, avocados, tomatoes, peanuts, and exotic fruits from subtropical regions.

they came under the direct scrutiny of the state, which meant that regular visits were paid to them by the curacas. And twice a year a home inspector known as a *llactacamayoc* came to ensure that the wife was properly feeding and clothing her family and maintaining personal hygiene.

Standards of cleanliness were high among the Incas. This was generally true of all the Andean peoples, although some had limited access to water for bathing. The Incas demanded that every wife guard the well-being of her family by not only maintaining dietary needs but also seeing to it that clothing, utensils, and bodies were reasonably clean. On inspection days, the reed mat hanging over every doorway had to be left open. The llactacamayoc would observe the housewife's cooking and washing and see how efficiently she had deloused her children—a task that involved crushing the tiny insects between her teeth or perhaps rubbing their heads with a concoction of *cebadilla,* or hellebore, a poisonous plant whose rhizome was dried and ground to a powder.

When a woman was judged to have been negligent of her household chores, she could be humiliated in front of the whole village by being forced to eat dirt taken from inside her home. The husband would have to do the same or else drink wastewater that had been used by the family for washing their bodies and hair. This dual punishment established the husband as having joint—or perhaps supervisory—responsibility for the household.

Under Inca law, marriage was for life. If a man threw out his wife, he was compelled to take her back. If he threw her out a second time, he was publicly punished. A third rejection could bring with it the risk of a death penalty, since Inca law made all acts of habitual disobedience a capital offense.

The Inca aristocracy was also subject to these strict marriage laws. A noble might do as he pleased with his "secondary wives," but he could not cast off his first, legitimate wife, or give her to another man. In some instances the penalties could be more severe for him than for the common man, if for no other reason than that the prestige of the nobility had to be upheld. With cases of murder, there was more of a double standard: The class the killer belonged to typically determined the punishment. A commoner lost his life, a curaca lost his job, and a noble lost face through a public reprimand.

Commoners were also liable to the death penalty for destruction of government property, and for lesser crimes when committed a second time. The last category included rape and the unauthorized moving of boundary stones delineating the lands of the emperor and religious institutions. These crimes were punished by the terrible *hiwaya*—the dropping of a heavy stone on the guilty party's back from a height of three feet.

One form of punishment aroused morbid fascination among the Spanish chroniclers who interviewed the Incas and recorded their laws. It was an ordeal, in Cuzco, in an underground labyrinth, known as the "place of the pit." This maze of tunnels and pits was lined with razor-sharp flints and had entrances through which, at any time, the official in charge might release snakes, scorpions, spiders, and even half-starved pumas. Those tossed into this hellhole were enemies taken in war who were especially hated and subjects who had directly threatened the Sapa Inca.

Although in the more routine cases citizens might be incarcerated while awaiting judgment, imprisonment was not a standard penalty for crimes, and the state had no buildings designated as jails. Normally, the punishments meted out were swift, immediate, and clearly defined. For example, thieves were whipped for the first offense, but persistent robbers met with harsher treatment—they were either banished to work on coca plantations in the Andean hotlands or suspended by the feet until dead. Murderers were hanged, stoned to death, or flung from a cliff.

In theory, the law-abiding citizen had nothing to fear from the Inca legal system. At the ayllu level, a curaca was empowered to deal with minor misdemeanors, but he had to refer the most serious cases to the Inca magistrates in the provincial capitals. Ultimately, only the Inca governor of a province had the authority to condemn

"PERUVIAN SHEEP": A TRIO OF EXOTIC, USEFUL BEASTS

A Spanish chronicler trekking through the former Inca realm in postconquest years encountered herds of bizarre animals that he called "Peruvian sheep." These creatures, he wrote, were "the size of a large deer, with long necks like camels."

The llama *(below, left),* which had so perplexed the foreign traveler, was indispensable to the local inhabitants. They ate the jerked flesh, called *charqui,* fashioned the hide into sandals, drums, and rope, and burned the animal's dried dung to heat their homes and cook their food. Peasants wove slings and sacks from the coarse wool.

Four feet high at the shoulder, this sturdy beast is the only native species large enough to be used as a pack animal and can carry as much as 100 pounds up to 20 miles a day. In addition to being valued for its many uses, the llama was revered in Inca theology and often sacrificed during religious rituals. Pure white llamas, kept by the Inca emperors, were prized for their beauty and served as an emblem of royal authority.

Like the llama, the alpaca *(below, right)* was domesticated long before the Incas' reign. Standing only three feet high at the shoulder, it was too small to

serve as a beast of burden but was prized for its rich, soft coat. Found only in the wild, the shorthaired, fawn-colored vicuna *(above)* is the smallest of the three and yields wool of such extraordinary luxury that when Inca weavers wove it into cloth, the garments made from it could be worn only by the elite.

an offender to death. The accused could call witnesses and conduct his or her own defense. Moreover, every citizen had the right to denounce injustices or abuses of power. It was the duty of the provincial governor to give the plaintiff a personal hearing, to investigate the charge, and to punish—usually with death—any official found guilty of corruption. And a roving inspector, the *tocoyricoc,* or "he who sees all," sent by the Sapa Inca, was supposed to ferret out abuses committed by the governor.

Remarkably few subjects openly rebelled or even broke the law. The Spaniards often remarked on the honesty and discipline of the people they saw. Indeed, this aspect so deeply impressed one conquistador, Mancio Sierra Lejesema, that he was moved to declare, in a testament drawn up in Cuzco in 1589: "Let it be known to His Catholic Majesty that the Incas governed in such a manner that among the Indians there was not a single robber, or vicious man, or lazy man, nor a perverse or adulterous woman." He also averred that "the Incas were obeyed and looked up to by their subjects as most capable beings and experts in the matter of government."

To keep out of trouble, the Incas believed their subjects need only follow their three golden rules—*Ama sua, ama lulla, ama quella,* meaning, "Do not steal, do not lie, do not be lazy." By adhering to them, every citizen could expect adequate support from birth until death. Thereafter, his or her destiny would be directly controlled by the gods.

Freestanding funerary towers, called chullpas, *dot the high mountain landscape near Lake Titicaca. Burial practices varied greatly from region to region within the empire and also from class to class. These tombs, belonging to local nobility, exhibit the finest coursed stonework, constructed without mortar. Since their construction nearly five centuries ago, they have suffered damage from both* huaqueros *and earthquakes.*

Two burial chambers cling to a sheer cliff rising above the Urubamba River between Pisac and Ollantaytambo. The rough pirca masonry identifies them as the resting place of humble peasants. But even the tombs of common folk fall prey to the depredations of the rapacious huaqueros; the buildings have been thoroughly ransacked, and only the stripped skeletons of the occupants remain.

The Incas had many gods, and their pantheon kept growing as new peoples and their idols were absorbed into the empire. Viracocha was venerated as the universal creator, but he had supposedly delegated day-to-day administration to such subsidiary powers as Illapa, the god of thunder, Pachamama, the earth mother, and Mama Quilla, the moon goddess. Chief among these deities was Inti, the sun god, from whom the emperors were said to descend, which made for a neat entwinement of Inti and Inca, church and state.

Ecclesiastical authority roughly paralleled the political hierarchy. The emperor appointed the Villac Umu, or head priest—usually a brother or other close relative—whose power was secondary only to that of the Sapa Inca himself. The head priest in turn selected Inca nobles to serve as bishops of the 10 religious districts into which the empire was divided. Priests below the bishops in the hierarchy typically came from the families of the curacas, the local officials. So diverse and numerous were the demands on the Inca religious establishment that at Cuzco's Coricancha, the Villac Umu headed a staff of more than 4,000 priests, priestesses, and other attendants.

There were fascinating similarities between Inca religious practices and Catholicism, which was to replace the ancient faith—conventlike houses for celibate women, colorful feast-day processions involving effigies held aloft for all to see, even a kind of communion, in which the priests ceremonially ingested food and chicha. Like the Catholic prelates, the Inca priests heard confessions, though not those of the emperor and his nearest kin, who took their sins directly to Inti, the sun god. Such similarities between the two religions helped to pave the way for Catholic missionaries.

Religious observances interrupted an otherwise rigid working routine, frequently for prolonged periods of time. In every month the Incas observed at least three feast days, and usually one major festival lasting for a week or more; together, these added up to some 120 days in every year. There were festivals to mark each new stage in the agricultural year, to celebrate the arrival of maturity and marriages, and to pay homage to the dead. And more were added when special circumstances, such as a drought, a famine, an earthquake, or the onset of war prompted the Sapa Inca to seek the intervention of the gods.

Although these extravagant public ceremonies reduced productivity and consumed vast amounts of food reserves, they were worth the price because they proved to be a major source of the Incas' political strength. Ties between the empire and its subject peoples were fortified, and the laboring masses were given reward and emotional outlet for their loyalty and industry. No less importantly, the festivals served to demonstrate the power of the Inca gods and to reinforce the authority of the beneficent Sapa Inca.

At these festivities, the emperor provided all food and drink, religious ritual, sacrifices, mock battles, music, and dancing. His officials also dispensed coca leaves, which provided a mild stimulant when chewed. Coca, from which cocaine is derived today, was viewed as a luxury, and nobles controlled its distribution.

In the first month of the rainy season, to mark the December solstice, the all-important Capac Raymi, or "magnificent festival," took place. During the first part of this celebration, *huarachicoy* maturity rites were carried out in Cuzco; so sacrosanct were these that non-Inca residents of the city had to leave its confines and remain at least six miles from its borders. With the rites over, the exiles returned, bearing fresh produce from the lands of the state and the religious establishment. But before they could take part in several days of feasting, drinking, and dancing that followed the huarachicoy, they had to exhibit their loyalty to the Sapa Inca by participating in a communion-like ritual in which they were offered, on silver and gold plates, cakes made of corn flour mixed with the blood of sacrificed llamas. Then, as Father Cobo reported, the priests told them, "What you have been given is the food of the Sun, and it will be

A THEOLOGY ROOTED IN THE NATURAL WORLD

The Incas ascribed metaphysical powers to a wide variety of objects, natural phenomena, and locales, including even mountains, which, among some Peruvian peasants today, continue to be revered. They referred to these essential icons of their religion by the generic expression *huaca,* or holy place.

The Spanish priest and chronicler, Father Bernabé Cobo, noted that the Incas made no distinction between the celestial and the terrestrial. The term *huaca,* he wrote, applied to "all of the sacred places designated for prayers and sacrifices, as well as to all of the gods and idols that were worshiped in these places."

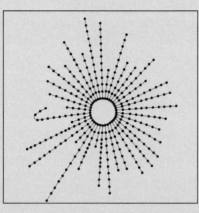

He listed 350 huacas—ranging from hills, rocks, and springs to ancient tombs and battlefields where past emperors had won glory—in the Cuzco area alone. Father Cobo also described how they were visualized as being grouped along a series of lines,

called *ceques,* which emanated from a single locus—the Coricancha in the heart of Cuzco *(diagram at left)*. Each of these ceques—and all their huacas—were the exclusive responsibility of a particular clan, which tended the grounds and offered sacrifices on proper occasions.

Archaeologists have determined that the location of some of the huacas correlates with the rising and setting of the sun on important days, and that thus they may have served as a kind of ritual calendar. But this conclusion, like so much else about a culture that left behind no written records, remains shrouded in conjecture.

Kenko is one of the largest huacas in the Cuzco region. A semicircular wall of smooth, coursed masonry accentuates the natural limestone monolith (left), *the centerpiece for religious ceremonies at the site. The adjacent cave* (above) *contains a carved altar.*

present in your bodies as a witness; if you ever were to speak evil of the Sun or of the Inca, this would be revealed and you would be punished for it." And all the people, said Father Cobo, duly promised that never in their lives would they do such a thing.

Modern-day excavations of Huanuco Pampa, the best-preserved of all Inca provincial centers, provide further insight into the importance the Incas attached to such festivals. Huanuco Pampa was a huge administrative city built on a flat plain about 13,000 feet above sea level, on the imperial highway from Cuzco to Quito, some 120 miles northeast of present-day Lima. On the site of this ancient ruin, archaeologists have uncovered the foundations of more than 3,500 structures within an area of about one square mile. All the buildings radiate outward from an enormous rectangular plaza, 600 yards long and 400 yards wide, dominated by a colossal raised platform, which is approached from the south by a monumental staircase. A series of formal gateways linked the central plaza to two smaller plazas and a compound of elaborate buildings, platforms, and artificial pools.

Taking note of the fact that the architecture was designed to provide huge open spaces and that myriad shards of pottery suggest heavy consumption of food and drink here, archaeologists have concluded that this city was more than just a base for administering a section of Tahuantinsuyu. It was, they believe, designed also as a ceremonial center, with space enough to accommodate between 10,000 and 15,000 individuals from the various ethnic groups in the region. Only one of many such centers throughout the provinces, Huanuco Pampa offered the Incas a chance to stage spectacular festivals that would expose subject peoples living far from Cuzco to the same awesome manifestations of Inca power as those living within a short radius of the Sapa Inca.

As the chroniclers describe them, pious rituals and sacrifices opened every festival, for, it was said, only after allaying their fear of supernatural powers could the people gradually abandon themselves to merriment. The process was spurred by the custom of frequent toasts; prodigious quantities of chicha were thus consumed. Cieza de

León stressed this aspect when describing the Hatun Raymi festival marking the end of the harvest of potatoes, corn, quinoa, and oca: "After having eaten and drunk repeatedly, and all being drunk, including the Inca and the high priest, joyful and warmed by the liquor, the men assembled a little after midday and began singing in a loud voice songs and ballads that had been composed by their forebears."

Thus, under the friendly influence of chicha, the different ethnic groups of Tahuantinsuyu became as one people—citizens who shared a love of storytelling, and who, above all, liked to express themselves in song and dance. Every province of the empire had its own distinctive repertoire of traditional dances, most, if not all of them, of a ritual nature. And rarely would anyone dance without also engaging in hypnotic, chantlike singing.

Father Cobo, visiting the province of Collao after the conquest, counted 40 different dances at a festival. He saw a jumping dance performed by men who wore masks and carried animal skins, a farmer's dance by men and women bearing agricultural implements, and one, still more colorful, "danced by both men and women with their faces painted and a gold or a silver ribbon across the nose

Once the scene of revelry, the Inca complex at Huanuco Pampa served as the administrative center for the surrounding region. The large open plaza could accommodate huge crowds for festivals and religious ceremonies conducted from the usnu, *a stone platform* (center). *Chicha played a major role in every observance; celebrants would imbibe the heady brew from a ceramic ceremonial kero* (left).

A pan flute, made of several unequal lengths of cane or reed lashed together, provided music for festivals and the imperial court. Its haunting, breathy tones are still closely identified with the mountainous region once ruled by the Incas.

145

from ear to ear; the tune was played on the dried head of a deer whose horns served as a flute. One dancer led off the dance and the others followed with perfect rhythm."

The music came from an astonishing array of percussion and wind instruments, as historical references and relics unearthed from graves demonstrate. There were drums and tambourines of several kinds, and also flutes of many shapes, sizes, and designs, carved of bone or made of reeds, including the popular *quena,* a length of cane pierced with as many as eight finger stops. In addition, there were multiple flutes, or panpipes, some made of five or more reeds bound together, others modeled in clay, and a few rare ones fashioned from the enormous pinions of the condor. Besides these instruments, graves have yielded an extraordinary range of trumpets, made from shells, gourds, and wood.

In addition to dancing and singing, festivalgoers listened with pleasure to the recitation of colorful narrative poems that had been passed from one generation to the next through constant oral repetition. The bulk of this literature consisted either of official epic poetry that effusively extolled glorious deeds in the nation's history, or religious poetry in the form of prayers and hymns, mainly in praise of Viracocha, the god of creation. Traditional romantic ballads, generally involving tales of unrequited love, freighted with nostalgia and filled with rich allusions to nature, were also popular.

Some of the epics continue to be told—in updated versions. One of these is the myth of Inkarri, a god said to be the son of the sun. In some of the tellings, he becomes a victim of Spanish aggression—tortured and then beheaded. But in today's account his head stays alive, hidden in a secret place, where it is growing a new body. When the body is complete, so the story goes, Inkarri will return to restore the Inca civilization to its former splendor.

There are perhaps 13 million Andeans in the modern republics of Peru, Ecuador, and Bolivia who may be regarded as descendants of the peoples of Tahuantinsuyu. Not only do five-sixths of them speak Quechua, the language that the Incas made the official *runa simi*—"man's speech"—of the empire; there are also many persons who see their world as being divided still into four quarters. Their belief in a restoration of Inca power and glory is most strikingly evinced by the reenactments of the death of the Inca emperor carried out each year by many indigenous communities in the Andes. In all these performances, the Sapa Inca is not garroted, as was Atahualpa, but beheaded like the legendary Inkarri. The significance of the change is that it reinforces the identification of the Sapa Inca as the son of the sun, and by linking him directly with Inkarri, suggests that he too is a Messianic redeemer.

Like the fabled Inkarri, some features of Inca life are now undergoing revival. Inca-built waterworks, long ago abandoned, are being redeveloped to irrigate barren lands, and ancient terraces are being reclaimed. And in a twist, the Incas even exert a new influence on the world as the foods of Tahuantinsuyu are discovered and eaten far beyond the empire's old borders. It is one of history's ironies that the most precious item found by the Spaniards when they invaded Peru was not gold or silver, but the humble potato. Today the world's potato harvest, in a single year, is worth many times the value of all the glittering metals looted from the Inca empire by its Spanish

In the same manner as her ancestors, a modern-day Andean woman in traditional dress gathers salt from one of the many evaporation pans cut into the watercourse of a saline stream. The age-old work ethic of the region—so brilliantly harnessed by the Incas—survives among their descendants and reflects the abiding heritage of the glittering, bygone empire.

conquerors. But now agriculturalists are focusing their attention on other produce commonly consumed in Inca times. Among the long-neglected crops having a resurgence is quinoa, which contains up to 50 percent more protein than rice, wheat, or corn. It is being distributed widely and has begun to appear in American supermarkets. The non-Andean world is also showing interest in *arracacha,* a distant relative of the carrot, which combines the tastes of celery, cabbage, and roasted chestnuts; amaranth, a plant with spinachlike leaves and myriad protein-rich seeds that, when heated, burst open like nutty popcorn; and *nuñas,* a remarkable variety of bean with the flavor of roasted peanuts. Oca, similar to the sweet potato, has become popular in New Zealand, and cherimoya, a fruit once prized by the Incas, is now grown commercially in California.

The proud past is gathering renewed strength in the hearts and minds of young Andeans. Peruvian schoolchildren learn to recite the rhythmical list of rulers of the Inca dynasty, chanting "Manco Capac, Sinchi Roca, Lloque Yupanqui, Mayta Capac, Capac Yupanqui, Inca Roca, Yahuar Huacac, Viracocha, Pachacuti, Topa Inca Yupanqui, Huayna Capac, Huascar, Atahualpa," names that call forth images of a creative, orderly people who became a constructive force of boundless energy and heroic achievements.

LIVING DEAD OF THE ANDES

As early as 4000 BC, there were Andean peoples who mummified their dead. Perhaps they were simply copying nature, since many lived near coastal deserts where corpses resisted decay for millennia, preserved by the arid climate alone. The mummy bundle shown above is one of these, found in 1896 on the Peruvian coast near Lima by the German archaeologist Max Uhle. Within lies a 12-year-old girl, confined in a basket covered by a woven woolen shroud, where she had remained almost intact for more than 500 years. Her family had simply placed her body, carefully wrapped but unembalmed, in extremely dry soil.

Such models of natural preservation bolstered the practice of ancestor worship that took hold as societies grew increasingly complex. Some communities began using artificial techniques to keep the bodies of clan elders or deceased chiefs in a lifelike state. These mummies played a ceremonial role during religious rites.

sessors, who would consult mummified relatives on practical and moral issues.

Today, Andean mummies speak volumes about the world in which they lived. Some, shipped to high-technology laboratories, have been examined with techniques at the cutting edge of science. In the early 1980s, for example, American forensic scientists, using chemical analyses of hair samples, developed methods for determining whether a person had ingested cocaine. Cocaine is derived from coca leaves, which the Incas chewed to relieve fatigue. Successfully employing these techniques, which were developed for use in law enforcement, a team of four pathologists and an anthropologist tested for traces of coca in the hair of 163 mummies from different regions. They discovered that coca-leaf chewing had been widespread throughout the Andes. The team is continuing the study in order to follow the practice back to its presumed origins in Ec-

The mummies of a group of Inca emperors and their wives were shown to the early Spanish-Inca chronicler El Inca Garcilaso de la Vega in 1570, leading him to observe: "It must be supposed that they were prepared in some way, for bodies, dead for so many years, could not be so entire, and so covered with flesh, without the application of something to preserve them." He assumed that they had been taken high into the mountains and left for a period of time to dry out in the cold, thin air. He learned from another priest, who had examined the mummies, that bitumen, a tarlike substance, had been used to protect the leathery skin.

Garcilaso's report was only an educated guess, since the Incas never revealed their embalming secrets. What is known is that most of the mummies found, either predating the Incas or under their rule, were naturally dried, and that only in a few cultures were artificial methods used. Some early groups deliberately chose burial sites in desert coastal regions or in the dry, high plains. Others assisted nature by curing bodies over a fire. There were peoples who simply eviscerated their corpses; some took the process farther and filled them with plant materials, and others included treatment with resins, oils, and herbs.

Numerous mummies, dating from about AD 400, were found on the south coast of Peru, wrapped in four layers of cotton cloth. One scholar has suggested that each of these shrouds may symbolize a separate burial of the same corpse, reflecting a pre-Inca belief that there were four stages on the deceased's journey to heaven. The layers of fabric that tightly enveloped the cadaver functioned like a wick, drawing off fluids.

The burial style of a bundle indicates the status of the deceased. Regional nobles were interred in multiroom sepulchers with their possessions, and often with their wives, retainers, and slaves. Commoners generally ended their days in simple graves in the community's outlying fields, securely wrapped, surrounded by the few objects of value they had owned in life.

Some 5,000 years ago, on the north coast of Chile, the child above was prepared for burial. After the internal organs were removed, the trunk, arms, and legs were braced with sticks. Coated with clay, the body was then swathed in the skins of birds and topped with a wig made of human hair.

Shell inlays create haunting eyes that stare from the false head attached to a Pachacamac mummy bundle 800 to 1,200 years old. Textiles and feathers form the headdress. Adding such a head, or a mask, gave the packets a more human appearance and enabled the living to relate more comfortably to the dead.

Draped in a cloak of plumes and shod in sandals of wool and leather, this mummified man was 35 years old when he died. His gold adornments, including a crown, earrings of feathered wooden birds, and a mouthpiece decorated with serpents, signify their owner's royal status. He stood five feet, eight inches tall when he lived, sometime between the third and seventh centuries AD.

A stretcher bound to the third shroud (below) reinforced the bundle, making it easier to carry. Its poles, each nearly three feet long, had once served as beams for a so-called backstrap loom, probably belonging to the dead woman.

Bound in a knotted net bag of plant-fiber rope, the mummy bundle above appears as archaeologist Karen Stothert first saw it. Observing two distinct styles of knotting, she determined that more than one person made the bag.

Lifting the third shroud revealed a cloth parcel, ears of corn, gourds, and several distaffs. Among the contents of the work-basket, in the center, were no fewer than 59 colorfully decorated spindles.

A bowl, painted black (above), and a ceramic figurine (below, left), found in a workbasket within the third shroud, were instrumental in determining the age of the mummy. Their stylistic similarity to well-established Inca artifacts helped the archaeologists deduce that the woman's burial took place during the period of the Inca empire, between 1476 and 1532. Inside the bowl are chunks of a mineral used to fix dyes

So intricately assembled was the mummy bundle of a woman uncovered near the town of Ancón, Peru, in 1976, that it took the archaeologists Karen Stothert and Rogger Ravines almost two full days to reach the skeleton within. It was a huge bale, weighing more than 150 pounds, buried during the time of the Incas.

By noting what was found in each layer as she carefully removed the four shrouds, Stothert could reconstruct the original burial procedure. Dressed in a sleeveless tunic, the woman had been placed on a large piece of cloth with her head resting on a cotton-stuffed pillow and her bare feet tucked into a cross-legged position. Three rings—two of metal and one of beads—adorned her hands, which were laid across her chest.

Atop her body was a wicker workbasket containing a weaving kit filled with cones of cotton fiber, a wooden bobbin decorated with carved monkeys, 14 painted spindles, a distaff, and various dyestuffs. Small cloth parcels surrounding the corpse held corn, fruits, and beans, eight silver rings, and a *spondylus* shell from Ecuador, 600 miles away. A handful of coca leaves had been placed under her head.

All this had been arranged on the first shroud—a beige fabric with green and maroon stripes—before it was folded tightly across the body and sewn shut. The parcel was then packed with leaves and enclosed inside a second

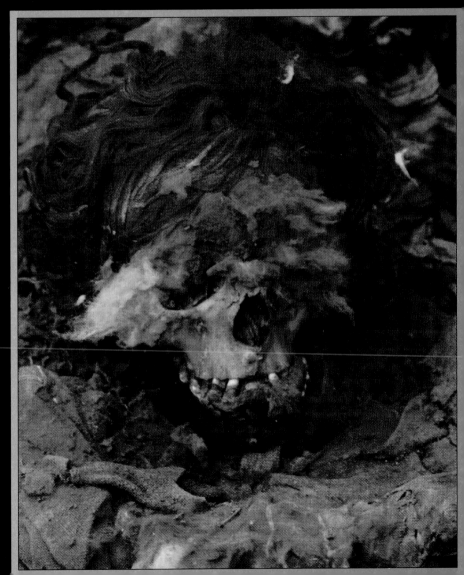

Subjected to forensic autopsies, x-rays, and electron microscopes, Andean mummies have yielded surprising information. Samples of their soft tissues, when rehydrated, have even enabled scientists to identify diseases that afflicted the peoples of this region throughout their history. Defying conventional wisdom, mummy studies revealed that when Andean civilization shifted to agriculture, health did not improve but declined. Hunter-gatherers were not stricken with many of the illnesses that plagued their descendants, and early cultures had a child-mortality rate roughly half that of later populations. As nomadic groups settled into sedentary societies, sanitation problems led to an increase in tuberculosis, pneumonia, and intestinal parasites.

Verified also is the terrible toll exacted by European-borne smallpox, measles, typhus, cholera, yellow fever, and bubonic plague—which killed an estimated 95 percent of the Inca population. But a tantalizing question goes unanswered. Was syphilis brought to Europe from America? There is evidence that the organism causing it existed in the New World prior to the Spanish conquest, whereas the disease was unknown in Europe before 1492.

On the new research frontier of molecular archaeology, scientists have found a way to isolate, in the tissues of mummies, DNA—the chromosome molecule that transfers genetic characteristics in all life forms. As they replicate the DNA, these pioneers are looking both for family

Lung tissue, 1,300 years old, was taken from this mummified Nazca boy (right), then rehydrated in the laboratory. Bacteria found were tested to reveal that the child had suffered from tuberculosis, which had affected his liver, kidney, and spine, causing the curvature in his back.

The first recorded case of hookworm infestation in the Americas was that of this Tiahuanaco mummy (right), dating from sometime around AD 900. Using a scanning electron microscope, pathologists discovered hookworms attached to the interior of the mummy's small intestine.

It had long been suspected that the Incas practiced human sacrifice after such momentous events as earthquakes or great military victories. Early chroniclers, however, presented contradictory accounts, and scholars hotly debated the question for centuries. Then, archaeologists found indisputable evidence of the fact in a collection of mummies.

Many early Catholic missionaries reported tales of youngsters who were strangled, had their throats slit with an ornate ceremonial knife called a *tumi,* or were left to die of exposure high in the Andes, their deaths assuring community welfare and bringing great honor to their families. Father Bernabé Cobo wrote that 200 children had been sacrificed to celebrate an emperor's coronation. Perhaps it was in reaction to Spanish use of these grisly anecdotes to justify conquest and forced conversion that Garcilaso de la Vega denied that such "barbarian ceremonies" existed among his mother's Inca ancestors.

Only in 1897 did the first solid clues of such rites appear. While excavating a cemetery at the Inca-built sun temple of Pachaca-mac, Max Uhle found the remains of a group of young women— buried with an array of Inca objects—who "did not die a natural death, but were victims of strangulation." He concluded that they were priestesses of the sun god, Inti, and that they had been ceremonially slain. Then, starting in 1954, a series of finds high in the southern Andes revealed the prowess and dedication that the Incas put into these deadly devotions. At heights that challenge the best-equipped modern expeditions—for example, near the 17,815-foot summit of Chile's Cerro el Plomo and on the Cerro Aconcagua in Argentina—climbers stumbled upon burial chambers holding the richly bedecked bodies of youths, dead for five centuries but perfectly preserved by the year-round cold. Some archaeologists believe that through these mountain sacrifices the Incas combined appeasement of the local mountain deity with worship of Inti, thus gaining respect for their own religion.

At each of these locations, 500 years ago, Inca priests and worshipers, having chosen a highborn youngster of flawless beauty, had walked with the child to a hallowed pinnacle. They carried firewood, stones to build the burial chamber, and artifacts to place in the young victim's grave. Some of the mummies wore expressions of untroubled repose, leading archaeologists to conclude that the youngsters had been first intoxicated with *chicha,* then buried alive. Before the alcoholic stupor faded, they had frozen to death.

Bent in a fetal position, the seven-year-old boy found on Aconcagua was wrapped in a cloak of yellow macaw feathers and several embroidered blankets. His body was painted red, a symbol of life, and he had been dressed in a wool tunic and sandals and adorned with a necklace made of stone beads.

Among the objects found in the grave of the boy of Aconcagua was a diminutive two-inch figure of a male (left) *and a small plume* (above).

El Plomo's eight-year-old (right) wears a
headdress of condor feathers, an alpaca
cloak, silver ornaments, and red face
paint. Vomit stains his tunic where he
threw up beer given to numb his senses.
Found with him (foreground) were
a bag of coca, figurines of a woman
and two llamas, and pouches of
the youth's own baby teeth,
nail parings, and hair.

A FLOWERING OF CULTURES

Long before the Incas came to dominance, several different cultures flourished in the Andean region. The first hunters and fishers arrived at least 12,000 years ago, and by 3000 BC, fishing villages dotted the arid coast, and small farming communities were springing up in the desert oases and in the fertile valleys of the Andean foothills.

A millennium later, larger social groupings moved inland, over the peaks, settling on the forested eastern slopes and using irrigation methods that had been developed on the coast to water their crops. Population centers grew up around temple complexes, and artisans began turning out pottery and textiles of increasing sophistication.

Archaeologists classify Andean artifacts by time period and geographical distribution. They use the term *horizons* to identify major phases of stylistic unity, broken down by the similarities that the objects display in their aesthetics and technology.

EARLY HORIZON: 1400-400 BC

STAFF GOD

Named for the temple center at Chavin de Huantar, in a small northern valley on the eastern slopes of the Andes, the Chavin style—tied to a powerful new religion—emerged around 1400 BC and reached the peak of its influence by 400 BC.

Believed to have been focused on an oracle who allegedly could see the future, fight disease, and petition the gods, the religion, or cult, gradually spread south. It reached the area of modern Lima by 1000 BC and Ayacucho, more than 200 miles farther inland, by 500 BC. Priests may have been sent from Chavin de Huantar to teach communities to worship Chavin deities like the feline or staff god *(above),* so named for the rod he holds.

The Chavin people made several major technological advances. They introduced the loom and experimented with metallurgic techniques, such as soldering, welding, and alloying gold and silver. Among the items they produced were large metal sculptures and yarn-dyed fabrics with painted designs of such icons of the Chavin cult as a god with a grinning jaguar face and animals found in the Amazon lowlands.

EARLY INTERMEDIATE PERIOD: 400 BC-AD 550

MOCHE VESSEL

Distinctive regional styles began to emerge on Peru's southern coast. Two notable features of the so-called Paracas culture of the Paracas Peninsula were its beautiful textiles and its bottle-shaped shaft tombs, each with room for at least 40 bodies.

Another people, the Nazca, farmed valleys 200 miles south of present-day Lima. By 370 BC, a Nazca style dominated the southwestern coast, leaving its mark particularly on ceramics. The Nazca are famous for the puzzling Nazca lines—huge ground drawings made by scraping away stones and gravel to reveal the lighter-colored earth beneath, then piling these stones along the edges. The lines are most likely an expression of the Nazca religion.

On the northern coast of Peru, the warlike Moche culture arose about 100 BC and spread its control more than 150 miles along the coast. The Moche developed a complex metallurgy, monumental buildings made of adobe, and an elaborate art style—expressed significantly in vessels that bear realistic portraits *(above).*

MIDDLE HORIZON: AD 550-900

STAFF GOD SCULPTURE

Now dawned the age of great cities. At 12,500 feet, on the shores of Lake Titicaca, pyramids and stone temples rose, decorated with fine carvings such as that of the god *(above)* thought to be an interpretation of the old Chavin staff god. The people who built these edifices settled the site around 1000 BC and began to construct the city of Tiahuanaco about AD 100.

By AD 500, the Tiahuanacans dominated the southern Andes, disappearing about 500 years later. During their hegemony they established faraway colonies, reclaimed land from around the shores of Lake Titicaca, and sent llama caravans to trade along the coast.

Meanwhile, Huari, a settlement 600 miles to the north, was growing into a city. At its height it had between 35,000 and 70,000 inhabitants, whose houses were served by an underground water system. Weaving counted as one of the culture's artistic traditions. When the Huari people vanished around AD 900, they left a major legacy—the concept and institutions of the imperial state.

LATE INTERMEDIATE PERIOD (COASTAL): AD 900-1476

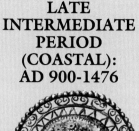

GOLDEN TUMI

LATE INTERMEDIATE PERIOD (HIGHLAND): AD 900-1476

KILLKE PITCHER

LATE HORIZON: AD 1476-1532

INCA FIGURE

EARLY COLONIAL PERIOD: AD 1532-1572

PIZARRO PORTRAIT

Collapsing empires ushered in a time of strife as smaller groups, emboldened by the Huari example, tried their hand at empire building. Starting from the former Moche heartland on the northern coast of Peru, the Chimu gradually incorporated 600 miles of coastline into their realm. From Chan Chan, their well-irrigated desert capital of 36,000 inhabitants, the lords of Chimu ruled a society of rigid classes, where highly skilled artisans enjoyed special favor.

The Chimu empire was supported by complex irrigation and enriched by conquest of such neighboring cultures as the Chancay, the Ica-Chinca, and the Sican. Sican art is represented above by a ceremonial knife. At their peak the Chimu adorned their clothing and household articles with intricately worked gold, wove precious textiles of surpassing beauty, and vied for power with their highland Inca rivals.

Descended from a people who had settled in the valley of Cuzco, more than 11,000 feet above sea level, the Incas did not develop a distinctive culture until AD 1200, signified by the pitcher above. Although Cuzco, their capital, had begun to expand, their power remained local. Then, in 1438, Pachacuti Inca Yupanqui took the throne. Calling himself Earthshaker, he marched through the Andes conquering, negotiating, and forging a string of states into a single mighty empire. Pachacuti rebuilt Cuzco into a city of enormous stone palaces and temples and brought his numerous provinces under the direction of a single vast, well-functioning governmental bureaucracy. His son, Topa Inca, succeeded him in 1471, after having dealt the Chimu the defeat that secured Inca sovereignty over the entire region, from Ecuador to the heart of Chile.

Its power secured, the Inca culture soared to its zenith. A vast road system carried armies and rich trade. Goldworking, ceramics, and textiles reached new heights of beauty and technical perfection. Stonecutters executed massive, precision-hewn edifices. Inca nobles, like the one shown above in a golden statuette, ruled the Andes until the emperor Huayna Capac died of smallpox sometime between 1525 and 1527, followed shortly thereafter by his heir, leaving open the question of succession and setting off a civil war. The war ended in 1532 when one of Huayna Capac's two contending sons, Atahualpa, became the victor, and the other, Huascar, a prisoner.

By this time, the Spaniard Francisco Pizarro had made a fateful sighting of the Inca coast. With fewer than 200 men, the conquistador would take advantage of the civil war and smallpox epidemic raging through the empire to attack Inca troops, capture Atahualpa, and execute him.

Pizarro and his band advanced on Cuzco in 1533, and were overwhelmed by the city's unexpected beauty. They placed Manco Inca, Atahualpa's half brother, on the throne to rule as a Spanish puppet.

Soon afterward, Manco Inca led his people in an unsuccessful revolt. He was ultimately forced to flee Cuzco, where Pizarro ruled until he was murdered in 1541 by supporters of a rival. Within the year, a viceroy arrived in Lima to govern the Andean territories as provinces of Spain.

In 1545 the Spanish found and killed Manco Inca, still emperor to a few thousand Incas who had taken refuge with him in the jungle, where they built the city of Vilcabamba. Manco's son, Tupac Amaru, the last Inca emperor, held out until his base in Vilcabamba was overrun by the Spaniards in 1572.

ACKNOWLEDGMENTS

The editors wish to thank the following individuals and institutions for their valuable assistance in the preparation of this volume:

Ferdinand Anton, Munich; Arthur Aufderheide, Department of Pathology, University of Minnesota, School of Medicine, Duluth; Richard L. Burger, Peabody Museum of Natural History, Yale University, New Haven, Connecticut; Eve Cockburn, Paleopathology Association, Detroit, Michigan; Alana Cordy-Collins, Department of Anthropology, University of San Diego, San Diego, California; Christopher B. Donnan, Department of Anthropology, University of California, Los Angeles; Clark L. Erickson, Department of Anthropology/ University Museum, University of Pennsylvania, Philadelphia; Stuart Fleming, University Museum, University of Pennsylvania, Philadelphia; LaCynda Gibson, Andean Explorers Foundation and Ocean Sailing Club, Reno, Nevada; April Goebel, National Geographic Society, Washington, D.C.; Martha Hill, Peabody Museum of Natural History, Yale University, New Haven, Connecticut; J. L. Hollowell, Elkton, Maryland; Heidi Klein, Bildarchiv Preussischer Kulturbesitz, Berlin; Sue McIntyre, Arlington, Virginia; W. Iain Mackay, British Museum, Museum of Mankind, London; Susan A. Niles, Department of Anthropology and Sociology, Lafayette College, Easton, Pennsylvania; Calogero Panepinto, Milan; Lino Pellegrini, Milan; Sara Posey, Department of Ethnography, British Museum, London; Walter Reunig, Museum für Völkerkunde, Munich; Luisa Ricciarini, Milan; Royal Library, Copenhagen; Gene Savoy, Andean Explorers Foundation and Ocean Sailing Club, Reno, Nevada; Axel Schulze-Thulin, Linden-Museum Stuttgart, Stuttgart; Anthony Shelton, Department of Ethnography, Brighton Museum and Art Gallery, East Sussex; Charles Stanish, Department of Anthropology, Field Museum of Natural History, Chicago, Illinois; Karen Stothert, Department of Sociology and Anthropology, Trinity University, San Antonio, Texas; John W. Verano, Department of Anthropology, Smithsonian Institution, Washington, D.C.

PICTURE CREDITS

The sources for the illustrations in this volume are listed below. Credits from left to right are separated by semicolons; credits from top to bottom are separated by dashes.

Cover: Brian Moser/Hutchison Library, London; inset, Museum Rietberg, Zurich. End paper: Art by Paul Breeden. 6: Hans Silvester-RAPHO, Paris—American Museum of Natural History, photo R. P. Sheridan 3211(2). 8, 9: Yale University, Peabody Museum of Natural History, New Haven. 10, 11: Yale University, Peabody Museum of Natural History, New Haven; Yale Peruvian Expedition Papers, Manuscripts and Archives, Yale University Library, New Haven, photographed by William K. Sacco—Yale University, Peabody Museum of Natural History, New Haven. 13: Art by Stephen R. Wagner. 14: Musée de l'Homme, Paris; Thomas Gilcrease Institute of American History and Art, Tulsa. 17: Loren McIntyre, courtesy Museo e Instituto de Arqueología, Universidad de San Antonio Abad del Cuzco. 19-23: Gene Savoy, Andean Explorers Foundation and Ocean Sailing Club, Reno. Map by Gary Robert Buchanan. 27: Loren McIntyre. 28, 29: Photo, John Bigelow Taylor 1991/American Museum of Natural History; Archivo Oronoz, Madrid. 30, 31: Dr. Gordon McEwan/Denver Art Museum. 32: Archivo Oronoz/Museo de America, Madrid 4665. 35: W.P.S./Ricciarini, Milan. 36-38: Yale University, Peabody Museum of Natural History, New Haven. 39: W.P.S./Ricciarini, Milan. 40, 41: Yale University, Peabody Museum of Natural History, New Haven; Luisa Ricciarini, Milan. 42, 43: Yale University, Peabody Museum of Natural History, New Haven; Tom Owen Edmunds, London. 44, 45: W.P.S./Ricciarini, Milan. 46: Loren McIntyre. 48, 49: W.P.S./Ricciarini, Milan. 50: Servicio Aerofotografico Nacional. 51: Art by Stephen R. Wagner. 54: W.P.S./Ricciarini, Milan. 58, 59: Ferdinand Anton, Munich/Museo de la Universidad Cuzco; Det Kongelige Bibliotek, Copenhagen; Musée de l'Homme, Paris, photo D. Destable. 60: Neil Maurer—Foto Ferdinand Anton, Munich, private collection; from *Circa 1492: Art in the Age of Exploration*, Jay A. Levenson, editor, National Gallery of Art, Yale University Press, New Haven, 1991. 61: Dumbarton Oaks Research Library and Collections, Washington, D.C. 62: Loren McIntyre. 63: American Museum of Natural History, photo D. Finnin. 66, 67: Loren McIntyre/Amano Museum, Lima. 68, 69: Det Kongelige Bibliotek, Copenhagen. 71: Loren McIntyre/Museo e Instituto de Arqueología, Universidad de San Antonio Abad del Cuzco. 72, 73: Det Kongelige Bibliotek, Copenhagen. 75: W.P.S./Ricciarini, Milan. 76, 77: Background from *Inca Architecture* by Graziano Gasparini and Luise Margolies, Indiana University Press, Bloomington, 1980. Daniele Pellegrini, Milan (2)—Robert Harding Picture Library, London; Luisa Ricciarini, Milan. 78, 79: Background from *Inca Architecture* by Graziano Gasparini and Luise Margolies, Indiana University Press, Bloomington, 1980. Dr. Gordon McEwan/Denver Art

Museum (2). 80, 81: Background from *Inca Architecture* by Graziano Gasparini and Luise Margolies, Indiana University Press, Bloomington, 1980. ZEFA, London; © Wolfgang Kaehler. 82, 83: Background from *Inca Architecture* by Graziano Gasparini and Luise Margolies, Indiana University Press, Bloomington, 1980. W.P.S./Ricciarini, Milan; © Wolfgang Kaehler—Robert Harding Picture Library, London. 84: Loren McIntyre/Museo del Oro del Peru, Lima. 86, 87: Neg. no. 334600, courtesy Dept. of Library Services, American Museum of Natural History. 88-89: Ullstein Bilderdienst, Berlin—Johan Reinhard, La Paz, Bolivia. 90: Nicole Couture/University of Chicago, Dept. of Anthropology. 91: Flip Schulke/Black Star. 92, 93: All John W. Verano, except far left, Loren McIntyre/Museo e Instituto de Arqueología, Universidad de San Antonio Abad del Cuzco. 94, 95: Dumbarton Oaks Research Library and Collections, Washington, D.C.; Dr. Gordon McEwan, courtesy S.A.N. Peru; Art Studio, Milan. 96: Hans Silvester-RAPHO, Paris; art by Stephen R. Wagner. 98: Dr. Gordon McEwan/Denver Art Museum. 99: Loren McIntyre. 100, 101: Neg. no. 334811, courtesy American Museum of Natural History, photo George Johnson. 102: Dr. James S. Kus, Fresno—Dr. Gordon McEwan/Denver Art Museum. 103: John B. Powell—Dr. Gordon McEwan/Denver Art Museum. 104, 105: Dr. Elias Mujica—Loren McIntyre. 106: Francisco Hidalgo, Paris. 107: Metropolitan Museum of Art, Michael C. Rockefeller Memorial Collection, gift of Nelson A. Rockefeller, 1969, 1978.412.219 and 1978.412.160; far right, Lee Boltin. 108: Loren McIntyre/Museum e Instituto de Arqueología, Universidad de San Antonio Abad del Cuzco; from "Inka-Peru" (Vol. 2 of 1991 catalog), M.R.A.H. Brussels AAM 46.7.286. 109: Francisco Hidalgo, Paris; Bildarchiv Hansmann, Munich. 111: Michael Holford, London. 112, 113: Art by Stephen R. Wagner; © 1982 David L. Brill. 114, 115: Christopher B. Donnan; Michael E. Moseley (2)—G. Dagli Orti, Paris. 116, 117: Trans. no. 2574(2) (photo by Richard P. Sheridan), courtesy Dept. of Library Services, American Museum of Natural History—Alana Cordy-Collins; G. Dagli Orti, Paris (2). 118: Don Bleitz; Textile Museum, Washington, D.C. 119: Trans. no. 3420(2) (photo by Beckett/Hollembeak), courtesy Dept. of Library Services, American Museum of Natural History—Textile Museum, Washington, D.C., 91.729. 120, 121: Foto Ferdinand Anton, Munich/Museo de Oro, Miguel Mujica Gallo Foundation, Lima; Francisco Hidalgo, Paris (2). 122: Loren McIntyre. 125: Neil Maurer. 126: Linden-Museum Stuttgart, photo Ursula Didoni. 127: Art Institute of Chicago/photo by Robert Hashimoto. 128: Loren McIntyre/Garcilazo (Cuzco) (2). 129: Loren McIntyre/Amano Museum, Lima; Det Kongelige Bibliotek, Copenhagen. 130: Det Kongelige Bibliotek, Copenhagen. 132, 133: Dr. Gordon McEwan/Denver Art Museum; Derek Bayes/courtesy of the Trustees of the British Museum, Dept. of Ethnography; Loren McIntyre/Amano Museum; photo H. R. Dorig/Hutchison Library, London. 134: Photo H. R. Dorig/Hutchison Library, London (2). 136: Denver Art Museum. 137: Peabody Museum of Archaeology and Ethnology, Harvard University, photo by Hillel Burger—Neil Maurer. 138, 139: Loren McIntyre. 140: Daniele Pellegrini, Milan. 141: Wolfgang Kaehler Photography. 143: Art by Stephen R. Wagner—Dr. Gordon McEwan/Denver Art Museum (2). 144, 145: Denver Art Museum—Craig Morris, New York City—Linden-Museum Stuttgart, photo Ursula Didoni. 147: Dr. Gordon McEwan/Denver Art Museum. 149: University Museum, University of Pennsylvania, neg. no. T4-131c3. 150: American Museum of Natural History, photo by R. P. Sheridan 2647(2); University Museum, University of Pennsylvania, neg. no. G5-18588. 151: American Museum of Natural History, photo by C. Chesek, cat. no. B/7737; from "L'Or du Pérou," Fondation de l'Hermitage, Lausanne, 17 Juin-4 Septembre, 1988, photos by Francisco Hidalgo. 152, 153: Neil Maurer. 154, 155: Eve Cockburn. 156: Juan Schobinger. 157: Loren McIntyre/Chile's Natural History Museum, Quinta Normol, Santiago. 158, 159: Art by Paul Breeden.

BIBLIOGRAPHY

BOOKS

Adorno, Rolena. *Guaman Poma*. Austin: University of Texas Press, 1986.

Anton, Ferdinand. *The Art of Ancient Peru*. New York: G. P. Putnam's Sons, 1972.

Ascher, Marcia, and Robert Ascher. *Code of the Quipu*. Ann Arbor: University of Michigan Press, 1981.

Baudin, Louis. *Daily Life in Peru*. Translated by Winifred Bradford. New York: Macmillan, 1962.

Beals, Carleton. *Nomads and Empire Builders*. Philadelphia: Chilton Company, Book Division, 1961.

Beltrán, Miriam. *Cuzco: Window on Peru* (2d ed., rev.). New York: Alfred A. Knopf, 1970.

Bennett, Ross S. (Ed.). *Lost Empires: Living Tribes*. Washington, D.C.: National Geographic Society, 1982.

Bingham, Alfred M. *Portrait of an Explorer: Hiram Bingham, Discoverer of Machu Picchu*. Ames: Iowa

State University Press, 1989.

Bingham, Hiram. *Lost City of the Incas: The Story of Machu Picchu and Its Builders*. New York: Atheneum, 1971.

Brundage, Burr Cartwright. *Empire of the Inca*. Norman: University of Oklahoma Press, 1963.

Cieza de León, Pedro de. *The Incas*. Translated by Harriet de Onis, edited by Victor Wolfgang von Hagen. Norman: University of Oklahoma Press, 1959.

Cobo, Bernabé:
History of the Inca Empire. Edited and translated by Roland Hamilton. Austin: University of Texas Press, 1979.
Inca Religion and Customs. Edited and translated by Roland Hamilton. Austin: University of Texas Press, 1990.

Cockburn, Aidan, and Eve Cockburn (Eds.). *Mummies, Disease, and Ancient Cultures* (abridged ed.). Cambridge: Cambridge University Press, 1980.

Coe, Michael, Dean Snow, and Elizabeth Benson. *Atlas of Ancient America*. New York: Facts On File, 1989.

Cotterell, Arthur (Ed.). *The Encyclopedia of Ancient Civilizations*. London: Penguin Books, 1988.

Cottrell, Leonard. *Digs and Diggers: A Book of World Archaeology*. Cleveland: World Publishing Company, 1964.

Deuel, Leo. *Conquistadors without Swords: Archaeologists in the Americas*. New York: St. Martin's Press, 1967.

Disselhoff, Dietrich. *Daily Life in Ancient Peru*. Translated by Alisa Jaffa. New York: McGraw-Hill, 1967.

Engel, Frederic André. *An Ancient World Preserved*. New York: Crown Publishers, 1976.

The European Emergence: TimeFrame AD 1500-1600 (Time Frame series). Alexandria, Va.: Time-Life Books, 1989.

Garcilaso de la Vega. *The Incas: The Royal Commentaries of the Inca*. Translated by Marìa Jolas from the French edition, Alain Gheerbrant, editor. New York: Avon Books, 1971.

Gasparini, Graziano, and Luise Margolies. *Inca Architecture*. Translated by Patricia J. Lyon. Bloomington: Indiana University Press, 1980.

Hagen, Victor Wolfgang von. *The Desert Kingdoms of Peru*. Greenwich, Conn.: New York Graphic Society Publishers, 1965.

Hardoy, Jorge E. *Pre-Columbian Cities*. New York: Walker and Company, 1973.

Hawkes, Jacquetta (Ed.). *Atlas of Ancient Archaeology*. New York: McGraw-Hill, 1974.

Hemming, John:
The Conquest of the Incas. New York: Harcourt Brace Jovanovich, 1970.
Machu Picchu. New York: Newsweek Book Division, 1981.
Monuments of the Incas. Boston: Little, Brown and Company, 1982.

Huamán Poma de Ayala, Felipe de:
Letter to a King. New York: E. P. Dutton, 1978.
Nuevo Corónica y Buen Gobierno. Edited by Richard Pietschmann. Paris: Institute d'Ethnologie, 1936.

Hyams, Edward, and George Ordish. *The Last of the Incas*. New York: Simon and Schuster, 1963.

Hyslop, John. *Inka Settlement Planning*. Austin: University of Texas Press, 1990.

Jackson, Donald Dale, and the Editors of Time-Life Books. *The Explorers* (The Epic of Flight series). Alexandria, Va.: Time-Life Books, 1983.

Katz, Friedrich. *The Ancient American Civilizations*. Translated by K. M. Lois Simpson. New York: Praeger Publishers, 1974.

Kendall, Ann. *Everyday Life of the Incas*. New York: Dorset Press, 1973.

The Land of the Incas. Photographs by Hans Silvester, text by Jacques Soustelle. Translated by Jane Brenton. London: Thames and Hudson, 1986.

Lanning, Edward P. *Peru before the Incas*. Englewood Cliffs, N.J.: Prentice-Hall, 1967.

Leonard, Jonathan Norton, and the

Editors of Time-Life Books. *Ancient America* (Great Ages of Man series). New York: Time Inc., 1967.

Lewis, Brenda Ralph. *Growing Up in Inca Times*. London: Batsford Academic and Educational Limited, 1981.

Lumbreras, Luis G. *The Peoples and Cultures of Ancient Peru*. Translated by Betty J. Meggers. Washington, D.C.: Smithsonian Institution Press, 1974.

McIntyre, Loren. *The Incredible Incas and Their Timeless Land*. Washington, D.C.: National Geographic Society, 1975.

McKern, Sharon S. *Exploring the Unknown: Mysteries in American Archaeology*. New York: Praeger Publishers, 1972.

Marrin, Albert. *Inca & Spaniard: Pizarro and the Conquest of Peru*. New York: Atheneum, 1989.

Menzel, Dorothy. *The Archaeology of Ancient Peru and the Work of Max Uhle*. Berkeley: University of California, 1977.

Métraux, Alfred. *The History of the Incas*. Translated by George Ordish. New York: Schocken Books, 1970.

Morris, Craig, and Donald E. Thompson. *Huánuco Pampa*. London: Thames and Hudson, 1985.

Moseley, Michael E., and Kent C. Day (Eds.). *Chan Chan: Andean Desert City*. Albuquerque: University of New Mexico Press, 1982.

Murra, John Victor. *The Economic Organization of the Inka State* (Research in Economic Anthropology, Supplement 1). Greenwich, Conn.: JAI Press, 1980.

Niles, Susan A. *Callachaca: Style and Status in an Inca Community*. Iowa City: University of Iowa Press, 1987.

Oro del Peru. Photographs by Francisco Hidalgo, text by Aurelio Miro Quesada S. Banco de Lima and Editions Delroisse, 1981.

Parker, Geoffrey (Ed.). *The World: An Illustrated History*. London: Times Books, 1986.

Prescott, William H. *History of the Conquest of Mexico and History of the Conquest of Peru*. New York: Modern Library, n.d.

Reader's Digest. *Mysteries of the Ancient Americas.* Pleasantville, N.Y.: Reader's Digest Association, 1986.

Romé, Jésus, and Lucienne Romé. *Life of the Incas in Ancient Peru.* Translated by Peter J. Tallon. Barcelona: Editions Minerva, 1978.

Rowe, Ann Pollard. *Costumes & Featherwork of the Lords of Chimor.* Washington, D.C.: Textile Museum, 1984.

Rowe, John Howland. *Max Uhle, 1856-1944: A Memoir of the Father of Peruvian Archaeology.* Berkeley: University of California Press, 1954.

Rowe, John Howland, and Dorothy Menzel. *Peruvian Archaeology.* Palo Alto, Calif.: Peek Publications, n.d.

Savoy, Gene. *Antisuyo: The Search for the Lost Cities of the Amazon.* New York: Simon and Schuster, 1970.

Silverblatt, Irene. *Moon, Sun, and Witches.* Princeton: Princeton University Press, 1987.

Stierlin, Henri. *Art of the Incas and Its Origins.* Translated by Betty Ross and Peter Ross. New York: Rizzoli, 1984.

Stuart, George E., and Gene S. Stuart. *Discovering Man's Past in the Americas.* Washington, D.C.: National Geographic Society, 1973.

Viola, Herman J., and Carolyn Margolis (Eds.). *Seeds of Change.* Washington, D.C.: Smithsonian Institution, 1991.

Voyages of Discovery: TimeFrame AD 1400-1500 (Time Frame series). Alexandria, Va.: Time-Life Books, 1989.

Westwood, Jennifer (Ed.). *The Atlas of Mysterious Places.* New York: Weidenfeld & Nicolson, 1987.

Wurster, Wolfgang W. *Die Schatz-Gräber.* Hamburg: GEO, 1991.

PERIODICALS

Allison, Marvin J., Daniel Mendoza, and Alejandro Pezzia. "Documentation of a Case of Tuberculosis in Pre-Columbian America." *American Review of Respiratory Disease,* 1973, Vol. 107.

Allison, Marvin J., et al. "Case of Hookworm Infestation in a Precolumbian American." *American Journal of Physical Anthropology,* July 1974.

Angier, Natalie. "A 'Lost City' Revisited." *Time,* February 11, 1985.

Bingham, Hiram:
"Further Explorations in the Land of the Incas." *National Geographic,* May 1916.
"The Story of Machu Picchu." *National Geographic,* February 1915.

Bray, Warwick. "Agricultural Renascence in the High Andes." *Nature,* May 31, 1990.

Cartmell, Larry W., et al. "The Frequency and Antiquity of Prehistoric Coca-Leaf-Chewing Practices in Northern Chile: Radioimmunoassay of a Cocaine Metabolite in Human-Mummy Hair." *Latin American Antiquity,* 1991, Vol. 2, no. 2.

Denevan, William M. "Peru's Agricultural Legacy." *Focus,* April 1985.

Erickson, Clark L. "Raised Field Agriculture in the Lake Titicaca Basin." *Expedition,* 1988, Vol. 30, no. 3.

Fleming, S. J., and Kathleen Ryan (Eds.). "The Mummies of Pachacamac, Peru." *Masca Journal* (University of Pennsylvania), 1983, Vol. 2, no. 5.

Hagman, Harvey:
"The 'Cloud People' of Old Peru." *Washington Times,* June 6, 1989.
"Site of Ancient City Discovered in Peru." *Washington Times,* September 3, 1989.

Hyslop, John. "Investigating Inca Roads." *Americas,* May/June 1986.

"If You Died in Old Peru." *Natural History,* February 1938.

Keatinge, Richard W., and Kent C. Day. "Chan Chan: A Study of Precolumbian Urbanism and the Management of Land and Water Resources in Peru." *Archaeology,* October 1974.

Key, Hopemary Ann. "Ancient Surgery: No 'Holes' Barred." *Pacific Discovery,* Spring 1991.

"Lost and Found in the Andes." *Discover,* April 1985.

"The Lost City." *Time,* August 28, 1964.

McIntyre, Loren M.:
"The High Andes." *National Geographic,* April 1987.
"Lost Empire of the Incas." *National Geographic,* December 1973.

"The Mist Lifts in the Andes." *Newsweek,* February 11, 1985.

Moseley, Michael E.:
"Chan Chan: Andean Alternative of the Preindustrial City." *Science,* January 1975.
"Peru's Ancient City of Kings." *National Geographic,* March 1973.

Murra, John V.:
"Guaman Poma de Ayala." *Natural History,* September-October 1961.

Ortloff, Charles R. "Canal Builders of Pre-Inca Peru." *Scientific American,* December 1988.

Petrich, Perla. "The Return of the Inca." *Unesco Courier,* February 1990.

Protzen, Jean-Pierre. "Inca Stonemasonry." *Scientific American,* February 1986.

Roberts, Shauna S. "Molecular Archaeology: PCR Amplifies the Pace of Discovery." *Journal of NIH Research,* September/October 1989.

Rogan, Peter K., and Joseph J. Salvo. "Molecular Genetics of Pre-Columbian South American Mummies." *Molecular Evolution,* 1990, pp. 223-234.

Ruiz, Jesús F. Garcia. "A Labyrinth of Forms." *Unesco Courier,* July 1984.

Sattaur, Omar. "The Lost Art of the Waru Waru." *New Scientist,* May 12, 1988.

Schobinger, Juan. "Sacrifices of the High Andes." *Natural History,* April 1991.

"Skullduggery." *Scientific American,* June 1990.

Stevens, William K. "Scientists Revive a Lost Secret of Farming." *Science Times,* November 22, 1988.

Stothert, Karen E.:
"Corrections for the Published Descriptions of a Late Horizon Mummy Bundle from Ancon." *Ñawpa Pacha* (Institute of Andean Studies, Berkeley, Calif.), 1991, no. 19.
"Preparing a Mummy Bundle: Note on a Late Burial from An-

con, Peru." *Ñawpa Pacha* (Institute of Andean Studies, Berkeley, Calif.), 1978, no. 16.

"Unwrapping an Inca Mummy Bundle." *Archaeology,* July/August 1979.

Vietmeyer, Noel. "Gift of the Incas." *National Wildlife,* September/October 1984.

OTHER PUBLICATIONS

"The Andean Civilizations" (Vol. 2 of *Handbook of South American Indians,* edited by Julian H. Steward). Smithsonian Institution, Bureau of American Ethnology, Bulletin 143. Washington, D.C.: U.S. Government Printing Office, 1946.

Bauer, Brian S., and Charles Stanish. "Killke and Killke-Related Pottery from Cuzco, Peru, in the Field Museum of Natural History." *Fieldiana: Anthropology,* December 1990, no. 15.

Circa 1492: Art in the Age of Exploration. Edited by Jay A. Levenson. Catalog of an exhibition at the National Gallery of Art, Washington, D.C., October 12, 1991-January 12, 1992. New Haven: Yale University Press, 1991.

"Fabric of the Inca Empire: Traditions Suppressed by the European Invasion." Catalog of exhibition, July 13, 1991-January 5, 1992. Washington, D.C.: Textile Museum, 1992.

Hollowell, J. L. "Precision Cutting and Fitting of Stone in Prehistoric Andean Walls: Re-assessment of the Fortaleza, Ollantaytambo, Peru." Unpublished manuscript.

"Inka Peru: Indianische Hochkulturen durch Drei Jahrtausende"
(Vol. 2). Catalog of exhibition at Schlossmuseum Linz, May 12-December 8, 1991. Linz, Austria: Landesmuseum Linz, 1991.

"L'Or du Pérou." Catalog of exhibition at Fondation de l'Hermitage, Lausanne, Switzerland, June 17-September 4, 1988. Lausanne: Fondation de l'Hermitage, 1988.

Lothrop, S. K. "Inca Treasure." Los Angeles, 1938.

McEwan, Gordon. "An Introduction to Andean Art and Archaeology." Manuscript in possession of author, 1990.

Moseley, Michael E. "Peru's Golden Treasures: An Essay on Five Ancient Styles." Chicago: Field Museum of Natural History, 1978.

Michael E. Moseley, and Alana Cordy-Collins (Eds.). *The Northern Dynasties: Kingship and Statecraft in Chimor.* Proceedings of symposium held at Dumbarton Oaks, Washington, D.C., October 12 and 13, 1985. Washington, D.C.: Dumbarton Oaks Research Library and Collections, 1990.

Oro del Perù. Catalog of exhibition at the Palazzo dei Conservatori, Rome, November 1981-January 1982. Milan: Electa, 1981.

"Researchers Seek Understanding of Ancient Surgery." Press release, Smithsonian News Service, March 1990.

Sweat of the Sun, Tears of the Moon: Gold and Emerald Treasures of Colombia. Essays published in conjunction with exhibition at the Natural History Museum of Los Angeles County, July 4-September 6, 1981. Los Angeles: TERRA Magazine Publications, 1981.

MUSEUMS

Readers interested in viewing Inca objects will find outstanding collections in the following institutions.

EUROPE

Linden-Museum Stuttgart, Stuttgart
Museum für Völkerkunde, Berlin
Museum für Völkerkunde, Frankfurt
Rautenstrauch-Joest-Museum, Cologne
Rijksmuseum voor Volkenkunde, Leiden
Roemer- und Pelizaeus-Museum, Hildesheim
Staatliches Museum für Völkerkunde, Munich

PERU

Museo Arqueológico, Cuzco
Museo del Banco Central de Reserva, Lima
Museo del Oro del Peru, Lima
Museo Nacional de Antropología y Arqueología, Lima
Museo Nacional de la Cultura Peruana, Lima

UNITED STATES

American Museum of Natural History, New York
Art Institute of Chicago, Chicago
Brooklyn Museum, Brooklyn
Denver Art Museum, Denver
Dumbarton Oaks Research Library and Collections, Washington, D.C.
Metropolitan Museum of Art, New York
Peabody Museum of Archaeology and Ethnology, Cambridge
Textile Museum, Washington, D.C.
Thomas Gilcrease Institute of American History and Art, Tulsa

INDEX

de Soto, Hernando: 14, 18
Diablo Huasi: cliff tombs at, *23*
Dominicans: in colonial Peru, 48, 49
Duho: 134

E

El Niño: 116
El Torreón (temple): 13, *38, 39, 83,* 94
Erickson, Dr. Clark: experimental archaeology at Lake Titicaca sites, 107-108
Espíritu Pampa: 10, 34

F

Festival of the Sun: 71
Field Museum of Natural History (Chicago): 104
Food: amaranth, 148; *arracacha,* 148; cherimoya, 148; *chuño,* 136; corn, 127, 129, 135, *136-137;* enduring Inca legacy, 147-148; fish, 135, 137; meat, 135, 139; *nuñas,* 148; oca, 136, 148; potatoes, 108, 127, 135, 136, 147; quinoa, 108, 127, 135, 136, 148

G

Garcilaso de la Vega (El Inca): 100, 156; on Inca life, 61, 62-63, 64-65, 70-71, 126; on Inca skills, 64, 89-90, 105, 110; on Pachacuti, 53; on quipus, 66, 67; reliability as chronicler, 51-52; on royal mummies, 74, 150
Gate of the Sun (Tiahuanaco): 87, *90*
Gran Pajatén: *20, 21*
Gran Vilaya: 19, 20, 22; limestone ruins at, *23*
Guambo: rope bridge at, *69*
Gulf of Guayaquil: 95

H

Hahua Incas: 59, 61
Hatun Raymi festival: 145
Hatun Rumiyoc: stonework in, 89
Hispaniola: 12
House of the Princess (Machu Picchu): *38, 39*
Huaca del Dragon: restored friezes on, *114-115*
Huacas (holy places): 26, 43, *83, 143;* and *ceques, diagram* 143
Huairas: 110
Huaman Poma de Ayala, Felipe: 126; petition to Philip III, *68-69*

Huanca province: 135
Huanuco Pampa: excavations at, *144-145*
Huaqueros: 123, 124, 140, 141
Huaraca: 27
Huarachicoy maturity rites: 130, 142
Huari: 75, 87, 95, 158, 159; as cultural ancestors of Incas, 88-89; mosaic-backed mirror, *94;* wooden scepter, *95*
Huasca: 60
Huascar: *14,* 16, 32, 58, 74, 95, 148, 159; death of, 29; proclaimed Sapa Inca, 15
Huayna Capac: 14, 15, 32, 58, 148, 159; mummy of, 74
Huayna Picchu: 8, 13, *36-37*

I

Ica: irrigation activity at, 56
Ica-Chinca culture: 159
Illapa (deity): 141
Inca empire: agricultural economy of, 7, 99-100; army and weapons of, *27, 53, 68,* 137; ceremonial centers in, 144; civil warfare in, 14, 16, 28, 58, 74; conquest of Chimor, 87, 104, 109, 112; distribution of resources in, 61, 63, 64-65, 137; dynasty list of, 148; ethnic groups in, 65, 144, 145; expansion of, 20, 32, 51, 53-54, 59, 108; extent of, *map* end paper, 10-11, 65; geographical extremes in, 54-55; governance in, 55-56, 57-65; irrigation needs in, 100-101, *102, 103, 104-105;* mining operations in, 110; morality and discipline in, 140; political succession in, 15, 58; population of, 11, 33-34; rainfall, 55; resettlements in, 56-57; sanitation system for cities, *103;* smallpox, effects of, 14-15, 16, 28, 34, 58, 154; and Spanish conquest, 7, 11-14, 16-18, 24-26, 28, 31, *32,* 33-34; stonework construction, 47, *75-83,* 85, 89, 90-94; suspension bridges in, 98, *99;* system of roads in, 67-70, 85, 87, 94-95, *map* 96, 97, *98, 99,* 137; taxation in *(mit'a),* 61-64, 65, 99, 110, 127, 128. *See also* Incas
Inca Roca: 89, 102, 148
Incas: appropriation of technology from earlier ethnic groups, 85; artisans, life of, 63-64; *ayllu,* role of, 125-127, 138; childbirth, infants, and children, 129, *130,*

131; and Chimu artisans, 88, 109, 111, 119; daily activities of, *68, 69,* 124-128, *129;* dances, 145-146; diet, 135; domesticated animals of, *138-139;* earplugs, use of, 59; education, role of, 70, 130-131; engineering skills of, 7, 17, 67, *82,* 98, *99;* festivals, feasts, and public ceremonies of, 125, 129, 142-146; footwear, 128, 133; and gold, 50, 85, 88, 109, 120; housing for, 75, *78-79,* 89, 133, *134,* 135, 136-137; land allotments *(topos),* 126, 131; limited technology of, 11; marriage, 131-132, 137-138; and mathematics, 66; messengers *(chasqui),* 69, 70, 96, 98; metalwork by, 106, *108-109,* 110; modern descendants of, 146-148; mythic birthplace of, 35, 52; names, choice of, 130; nobility, 58-61, 137-138, 142; origins of, 52-54, 85; peasantry, 124-126, *127;* personal grooming, 108, 133, 137; poetry, 146; quipus, use of, 65-67; schooling for, 70-71; Spanish domination of native culture, 34, 47; tax-paying heads of household *(purics),* 126, 136; textiles as valued commodity, 29, 60; trading by, 12; trephination by, *92-93;* veneration for royal mummies, *72-73,* 74; work ethic of, 124-125, 128, 131, *147;* writing, lack of, 11, 51, 65
Inca Yupanqui: 50-51. *See also* Pachacuti Inca Yupanqui
Inkarri: myth of, 146, 147
Intervalley Canal: *102,* 104
Inti (deity): 11, 13, 24, 35, 43, 47, 48, 50, 56, 62, 70, 72, 141, 142, 156; and mythic origin of Incas, 52-53
Intihuatana (ritual stone): 13, *42, 43*
Inti Raymi: 42

J

Jauja: 16
Jetas: 76, 77

K

Kenko *(huaca): 143*
Kero vessels: *32, 144*
King's Group: 13
Kipling, Rudyard: 35
Kubler, George: on architecture and environment of Machu Picchu, 44

43, *83, 143;* Inca beliefs in after-
life, 136, 150; Inca deities, 11,
13, 24, 35, 43, 47, 48, 50, 56,
62, 70, 72, 103, 141, 146, 156;
Inca ecclesiastical hierarchy, 141;
Inca rituals, 47, 48, 156; Inca tol-
erance, 55-56; *mamaconas* (chosen
women), 39, 70, 71, 72; ritual
garments, 60-61; ritual stone *(intihuatana),* 13, *42, 43;* role of
mummification, 32; sacrificial rituals, 47, 108, 156; similarities between Catholicism and Inca beliefs, 141-142; springs, spiritual
significance of, 81; Tiahuanacan
deities, 87, *91, 158*
Rowe, John H.: and floor plan of
the Coricancha, 49
Royal Danish Library: 68
Rucanas: 64
Rumiñavi: 24, 28
Rumiqolqa: quarries at, 91
Rutuchicoy naming rites: 129-130

S

Sacred Plaza: temples in, 13, 40, 42
Sacsahuaman, temple of: *30-31, diagram* 51, *76,* 83, 88, 91; Spanish
battle for control of, 31, 33
Saihuite Stone: *62*
Sancho, Pedro: 47; Pizarro's secretary, 48, 89
Santo Domingo, church of: *48-49;*
and Inca ruins underneath, 47-50
Sapa Inca: 14, 56, 59, 64, 71, 125,
126, 138, 142, 144; appointed
inspectors of, 67, 140; ceremonial
harvesting work by, 127; and the
Coya, 58; as Messianic redeemer
for modern-day Indians, 146-147;
as military commander, 27; mum-
mies of, 32, 73, 74; prerogatives
of, 57, 60, 61, 62, 134; succes-
sion of, 15, 58; title of Inca rul-
ers, 11, 52
Sartiges, Count de: and search for
Vilcabamba, 19
Savoy, Gene: *19;* search for lost cities in the Andes, 19-23
Seville: gold-leaf altarpiece fashioned
from Inca metalwork, *28-29;* Inca
artwork transported to, 34
Si (Chimu moon goddess): 114
Sican culture: 159
Sierra Lejesema, Mancio: 140
Silverblatt, Irene: on gender roles in
Inca society, 72, 126
Sinchi Roca: 148
Skull cups: 16, *17*

Skulls: as evidence of Inca trephination, *92-93*
Smallpox: spread of in New World,
14-15, 34, 154
Spain: amazement over Inca achievements, 17, 47, 48, 85, 91, 140;
conquest of Incas, 7, 11-14, 16-
18, 24-26, 28, 31-34; and destruction of royal mummies, 74;
domination of native Inca culture,
32, 34, 47; failure to maintain
infrastructure of Inca empire, 99,
103, 110; gold valued by, 60,
147; Inca gold used to offset
mounting Spanish debt, 28, 34;
and Indian forced labor, 34, 110
Spanish Inquisition: 48
Spondylus shells: *116, 117, 153*
Squier, Ephraim George: 92; and
ground plan for Coricancha, 48-
49
Stothert, Karen: examination of
woman of Ancón mummy bundle,
125, 152, 153
Syphilis: possible origin of in New
World, 154

T

Taclla (foot plow): 127, *129*
Tahuantinsuyu (land of the four
quarters): 11, 33, 51, 59, 65, 94,
125, 144, 145, 146, 147. *See also*
Inca empire
Taino Indians: 12
Tambo Colorado: military garrison
at, *134*
Tambo Machay: Pachacuti's lodge
at, *81*
Tambos: 67, *69,* 99
Tambo-toco: mythic birthplace of
Incas, 35, 40
Temple of the Sun (Cuzco): 39, *48-
49*
Temple of the Sun (Machu Picchu):
38, 39, 83
Temple of the Sun (Ollantaytambo):
77
Temple of the Sun (Pisac): *80-81*
Temple of the Three Windows (Ma-
chu Picchu): *40-41*
Textiles: Chimu, 119; as commodi-
ties, *60-61,* 119; dyes for, 131,
133
Throne of the Inca: *83*
Tiahuanaco: 75, 90, 91, 158; exca-
vations at, 86-87, *88-89;* mummy
from, *155;* stonework at, 87, 89,
90; temple complex at, 87, 88
Ticlo Pass: 54

Tocoyricocs: 67, 140
Toledo, Viceroy Francisco de: 32
Topa Inca Yupanqui: 55, *69,* 104,
148, 159; and expansion of Inca
empire, 51, 54, 65, 87
Topos: 126, 131
Torquemada, Juan de: on Inca
craftsmanship, 110
Torreón: *See* El Torreón
Trujillo: pre-Inca sites near, 87
Tucumán: 95
Tumbes: Inca town of, 13, 16
Tumi (ceremonial knife): *106, 108,
156, 159*
Tupac Amaru: 159; execution of, 34
Tupu (ornamental) pins: *58,* 59, *132*

U

Uhle, Max: 49, *89;* mummy finds
by, *149, 150,* 156; and study of
pre-Inca cultures, 86-87
UNESCO: restoration advisers from,
49
University of California: 49
University of Pennsylvania: 107
Urcon: 52, 53
Urubamba River: 7, *8-9;* cliff tombs
at, *141;* Inca irrigation improve-
ments to, *102,* 105
Urubamba valley: 54, 79

V

Vicuna: *139*
Vilcabamba: 32, 97, 159; Bingham's
search for, 7, 9, 10, 19, 35; last
Inca stronghold, 19, 34; Savoy's
search for, 19
Vilcabamba range: 54
Villac Umu: 141
Viracocha (deity): 103, 141, 146
Viracocha Inca: 53, 148
Virgins of the Sun: 48, 72

W

White Cordillera: 54
Woman of Ancón (mummy): 128,
133; unraveling and scientific examination of, 124, *152-153*
Women: and childbirth, 127, 129;
in Inca society, 58, 59, 126, *127,*
128-129, 136, 137; Inca view of
Spanish women, 126; selection for
and life as priestesses, 71-73, 141
Wool: 47, 59, 71, 119, 133, 139

Y

Yacolla: 132-133
Yahuar Huacac: 148
Yale University: 8, 10, 44

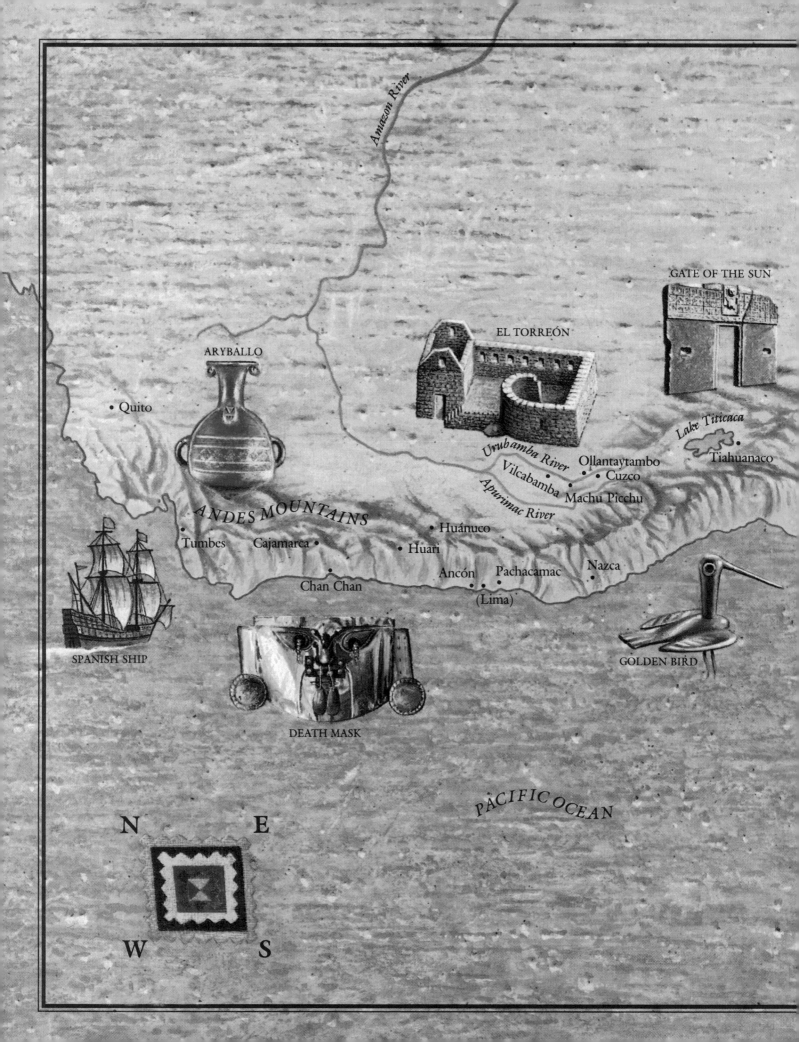

Amazon River

GATE OF THE SUN

ARYBALLO

EL TORREÓN

• Quito

Lake Titicaca

Urubamba River

Ollantaytambo

Tiahuanaco

Vilcabamba

Cuzco

Machu Picchu

Apurimac River

ANDES MOUNTAINS

• Huánuco

Tumbes   Cajamarca

• Huari

SPANISH SHIP

Chan Chan

Ancón   Pachacamac

Nazca

(Lima)

GOLDEN BIRD

DEATH MASK

PACIFIC OCEAN

N   E

W   S